FAITH
WALKING
through
SUFFERING & PAIN

FAITH WALKING

through

SUFFERING & PAIN

ELMER L. TOWNS

DESTINY IMAGE® PUBLISHERS, INC.
P.O. Box 310, Shippensburg, PA 17257-0310
"Promoting Inspired Lives."

This book and all other Destiny Image and Destiny Image Fiction books are available at Christian bookstores and distributors worldwide.

For more information on foreign distributors, call 717-532-3040.

Reach us on the Internet: www.destinyimage.com.

ISBN 13 TP: 978-0-7684-7178-6

ISBN 13 eBook: 978-0-7684-7179-3

For Worldwide Distribution.

1 2 3 4 5 6 7 8 / 27 26 25 24 23

CONTENTS

PART THREE

PART FOUR

Introduction

THE ETERNAL STRUGGLE WITH PAIN

N O one likes pain. Why? Because it hurts! Whether you talk about little pain or screaming suffering, people not only don't like pain ... some actually hate it!

When you think about suffering, remember what it does to you: crying ... grieving ... hurting ... agony ... miserable. These are only a few words that will disappear when you get to Heaven.

The apostle John did not see any pain when he looked into Heaven; he said, "God Himself will be with them. He will wipe away every tear ... no more death ... or sorrow ... or crying ... or pain. All these things will be gone forever. The One sitting on the throne will announce, 'Look, I am making everything new!' Do you want a new body? ... new life? ... new future?"

"Heaven's gonna be a wonderful place," my fourth-grade Sunday school teacher, Jimmy Breland, used to say. "Don'cha wanna go there?"

Yes, your pain will be gone when you get to Heaven because you will be with Jesus.

Jesus died to take away the penalty of sin so we won't be punished by God and we won't go to hell. So Jesus finished salvation. Wow! At the end of time, when we enter the "new Heaven and the new earth," Jesus will announce, "It is finished!"

What will be gone when you get into God's presence? No more suffering ... pain ... agony ... torture ... afflictions. He will also say "it is finished" to our present struggles with sin.

But let's come back to our present life on Earth. Let's talk about our struggles and pain. Remember, Jesus promised tribulation in the world: "I have told you all this so that you may have peace in me. Here on earth you will have many trials and sorrows. But take heart, because I have overcome the world" (John 16:33, NLT).

Why would Jesus promise suffering to His followers? Doesn't a worldly conqueror promise that his followers would have the spoils of victory, i.e., they could have all the loot they captured from their enemies? Also, conquerors promise their followers that they will eat the food of those they conquer, live in their houses—unrestrained freedom. But there is a contradiction here. Jesus is not a worldly conqueror. Jesus stands against murder, thievery, rape, self-indulgences. Jesus stands against all that worldly conquerors want. Jesus's kingdom is peace ... purity ... brotherly love ... happiness ... and worship. But with those pleasures come spiritual attacks and suffering.

Jesus understood the eternal struggle of satan against God ... of evil against good ... of deception against truth ... and selfishness against a God-centered life (notice, the initial violence is with satan and evil. He is the one in rebellion against God and righteous living).

Therefore, Jesus explained, "If the world hates you, remember that it hated me first" (John 15:18, NLT). Then He went on to explain, "Since they persecuted me, naturally they will persecute you" (John 15:20, NLT).

While God's kingdom is ruled by "faith, hope, and love—and the greatest of these is love" (1 Corinthians 13:13, NLT), satan's kingdom is ruled by the opposite, which is skepticism and unbelief; the opposite of hope is despair and fear. The opposite of love is anger, hostility, and hatred.

Notice what else rules satan's kingdom: There will be "worldly desires [lust] that wage war against your souls" (1 Peter 2:11). People will turn from God, "following the desires ... of their sinful nature" (Ephesians 2:3, NLT). They will continue as "evil doers" (1 Peter 2:12).

God knows all the types of evil that war against your world. The Bible says, "at that time you were without Christ, being aliens from the commonwealth of Israel and strangers from the covenants of promise, having no hope and without God in the world" (Ephesians 2:12). Because of past sins, the sinful habits they inspire, and their sinful nature, which is the source of individual evil, God gives two actions to the believer.

First, the believer is given a new nature to follow God. "Anyone who belongs to Christ has become a new person in Christ Jesus with new desires to follow God—old desires are passed away—and now has the possibilities of new things with Christ" (2 Corinthians 5:17, ELT).

But there is a second force God uses against any evil attack or evil desire within the believer: God allows suffering to conform the believer to Jesus Christ. Sometimes suffering comes from outsiders to persecute a child of God; at other times suffering comes from outside forces that put pressure (pain, suffering) on them. Whatever the source of suffering, the purpose of the believer's suffering is to make him more like Jesus Christ.

The apostle Peter, who went through many temptations and trials, tells us what suffering does to our faith: "trials will ... purify [your faith] as gold" (1 Peter 1:7, NLT).

James, the half-brother of Jesus and the leader of the Jerusalem church, explains that your sufferings will grow your faith: "Your faith is tested ... grows" (James 1:14).

Then Paul explains that your suffering will help you comfort others who suffer: "The Father ... comforts us in all our troubles, so we can comfort others. When they are troubled, we will be able to give them the same comfort God has given us. For the more we suffer, the more God will shower us with His comfort ... when we ourselves are comforted, we will certainly comfort you" (2 Corinthians 1:3-6, NLT).

But there is something else suffering accomplishes. When we suffer for our faith, we identify with Jesus in His suffering. "God calls you ... suffering just as Christ suffered ... follow His steps" (1 Peter 2:21).

One last thing about your pain and suffering: When you go through trials, you get God's attention. Because you identify with Jesus, God not only notices your suffering, but He also helps you in your pain. "Since He Himself has gone through suffering ... He is able to help us when we are tested" (Hebrews 2:17-18).

Why a book about suffering and pain? If you haven't suffered pain in the past, or if you are not suffering now, there will be a time in the future when suffering will come. This book will help you get mentally ready; but more than knowing about suffering, its purpose is to get you spiritually ready for your "time of trials."

PART ONE

FAITH
WALKING
through
SUFFERING & PAIN

Chapter 1

LEARNING FROM SUFFERING AND PAIN

These trials will show that your faith is genuine ...
tested as fire tests and purifies gold—though your
faith is far more precious than mere gold. So, when
your faith remains strong through many trials, it
will bring you much praise and glory and honor.

1 Peter 1:7, NLT

When troubles come your way ... you know your
faith is tested ... a chance to grow. So let it grow.

James 1:2,4

WHY would a loving God allow you to suffer pain? And why would a wise God let you go through physical torment, or even mental or emotional stress? As soon as we ask that question, remember that the pain issue did not begin with God. Pain was ignited by people—Adam and Eve; humans introduced pain to the world in which they lived.

God did not choose suffering! God chose the beautiful Garden of Eden to supply Adam and Eve with all the food they would need, both delicious and enjoyable. Everything needed was supplied. All they had to do was let God control and influence their lives. Then they could enjoy the Garden, plus fellowship with God at the end of the day, praising and worshipping Him.

Adam and Eve disobeyed God by doing what He told them not to do: " Of every tree of the garden thou mayest freely eat: but of the tree of the knowledge of good and evil, thou shalt not eat of it: for in the day that thou eatest thereof thou shalt surely die" (Genesis 2:16-17, KJV).

Notice two directives. First, they could eat any fruit they desired. It was good fruit that would make them healthy. But the second directive prohibited them from eating from one tree, with a warning that they would die the moment they ate that forbidden fruit.

What did God mean "thou shalt surely die"? A quick reading of this text would make the average person think God would strike them dead instantly. But they did not die when they ate the fruit. How long did Adam live? "So all the days that Adam lived were nine hundred and thirty years; and he died" (Genesis 5:5). No, Adam did not die instantly, but he began to gradually die physically. That is the way sin works on a person: gradually—influencing them spiritually, emotionally, and physically. Adam lived 930 years and then died physically.

But there is a second aspect of death when Adam ate the fruit. He died spiritually. His fellowship and "oneness" with God were immediately terminated. Adam and Eve could no longer enjoy fellowshipping with God in His presence.

Previously "they heard the voice of the LORD God walking in the garden in the cool of the day" (Genesis 3:8). As the couple made themselves available to God, He revealed Himself to them. What did they have? *The presence of God.* Now you on your knees can enjoy what Adam and Eve enjoyed in the garden; you can enjoy His presence as fully ...

completely ... openly as Adam and Eve. So, today, you can have a taste or touch of the presence of God. That taste is a future view of what you will enjoy in Heaven.

Because of sin, God introduced a new element of pain and suffering into the life of Adam and Eve. God first addressed the woman because she was the first to eat the forbidden fruit. "I will greatly multiply your sorrow and your conception; in pain you shall bring forth children; your desire *shall be* for your husband, and he shall rule over you" (Genesis 3:16). But pain was only the beginning of her suffering.

God also predicted for Adam, "Because you have heeded the voice of your wife, and have eaten from the tree of which I commanded you, saying, 'You shall not eat of it: Cursed is the ground for your sake; in toil you shall eat of it all the days of your life'" (Genesis 3:17). When God predicted sorrow for Adam, He said, "Both thorns and thistles it [the ground] shall bring forth for you, and you shall eat the herb of the field. In the sweat of your face you shall eat bread till you return to the ground, for out of it you were taken; for dust you are, and to dust you shall return" (Genesis 3:18-19).

Note carefully that they were not given pain; it was the by-product of their sin. They would have to work hard—toil and sweat—to get food to eat; their work would cause suffering and pain. They might enjoy sexual intimacy, but out of it would come a child, and its life would come through the pain of birth.

Did God send pain into the world? Can a good God send suffering on His people? Or did God allow consequences of their sin to cause pain for Adam and Eve? Did the results of their sin and disobedience cause continual suffering ... stress ... agony and pain?

JESUS DIED FOR OUR SINS

When Jesus was 30 years old, He went to the Jordan River where John the Baptist was baptizing. John the Baptist called people to repent and turn to God. Jesus did not need to repent nor turn to God. But John introduced Jesus to the world with the statement, "behold the Lamb of God who takes away the sin of the world" (John 1:29). Jesus would die for the sins of the world—including the results of pain, agony, separation, and isolation. Jesus would die for all and restore us to fellowship with God. That would give us access to eternal life with Him in Heaven. "In My Father's house are many mansions; if it were not so, I would have told you. I go to prepare a place for you. And if I go and prepare a place for you, I will come again and receive you to Myself; that where I am, there you may be also" (John 14:2-3).

JESUS PROMISED THAT HIS FOLLOWERS WOULD SUFFER TRIALS AND PERSECUTIONS

Jesus understood that His followers on this earth would suffer trials and tribulations. Why would they do that? Jesus said, "I have given them [followers of Christ] Your word; and the world has hated them because they are not of the world, just as I am not of the world" (John 17:14).

The world will persecute Christians because the world "offers only a craving for physical pleasures, and cravings for anything we see, and pride in our achievements and possessions" (1 John 2:16, NLT). Other religions of Scripture call these motivations "the lust of the eyes, the lust of the flesh, and the pride of life" (1 John 2:16, KJV). Those who live for these desires reject God the Father because the Lord of the universe is characterized by love, joy, and peace. Therefore people of the world take their vengeance out on Christians who follow the heavenly Father. Sometimes the world does not do it directly or immediately, but the ungodly will eventually persecute a Christian because of their allegiance to God. Jesus explains, "If the world hates you ... it hated Me first" (John 15:18, NLT).

When you begin following Jesus, the world will persecute you, just like they did Jesus. Jesus promised, "Since they persecuted Me, they naturally will persecute you" (John 15:20, NLT).

Peter challenged followers of Jesus to stay away from the influence of the world. "Dear friends, I warn you as 'temporary residents and foreigners' to keep away from worldly desires that wage war against your very souls" (1 Peter 2:11, NLT).

Why did Peter want followers of Christ to separate from evil? "They speak against you as evil doers" (1 Peter 2:12, KJV).

Notice the warning Paul gave the Ephesians about the source of strife and suffering: "You used to live in sin, just like the rest of the world, obeying the devil—the commander of the powers in the unseen world. He is the spirit at work in the hearts of those who refuse to obey God" (Ephesians 2:2).

WHAT SUFFERING ACCOMPLISHES

Pain hurts, and no one likes suffering. Going through trials can disorient us, and pressure can get us mentally discouraged. So why does God allow pain and suffering for His followers? Suffering can ultimately glorify God.

Peter writes to "God's chosen people," telling them, "By His great mercy ... we have been born again" (1 Peter 1:1,3). Then Peter encourages them, "God is protecting you by His power" (1 Peter 1:5). So he warns them, "There is wonderful joy ahead even though you have to endure many trials" (1 Peter 1:6, NLT). So why must they go through all these trials? "So when their faith remains strong through many trials, it will bring much praise and glory and honor on the day when Jesus Christ is revealed to the whole world" (1 Peter 1:7).

James, the half-brother of our Lord, wrote a letter to the early church telling them they would go through many trials in life. So James writes, "your faith will be tested" (James 1. While they may not understand why, the emotional pressure or physical pressure of trials resulting from suffering actually strengthens their inner person and ultimately strengthens their whole walk with Christ. Suffering grows faith.

Paul writes to the Corinthians explaining their many trials and difficulties. He wants their suffering to encourage others going through the same type of suffering. He writes, "God is our merciful Father and the source of all comfort. He comforts us in all our troubles so that we can comfort others. When they are troubled, we will be able to give them the same comfort God has given us ... For when we ourselves are comforted, we will certainly comfort you. Then you can patiently endure the same things we suffer" (2 Corinthians 1:3-6). Your suffering equips you to comfort others who suffer.

Peter wrote to remind the church that God calls us to do good, even if it means suffering: "... just as Christ suffered for you. He is your example, and you must follow in his steps" (1 Peter 2:21, NIV). Christ suffered for us—not only intense mental suffering, but also physical suffering that led to His death. How can we who follow His example expect a different kind of response from the unsaved world? So Peter reminds us that we have been called to suffer just as Christ suffered; He is our example and we follow His steps.

God has a purpose in your suffering. Remember, Jesus suffered, but God had many purposes why He allowed His Son to suffer. Technically, one accomplishment of Christ's suffering was that it was the ending of

His life. But Jesus's suffering was also the beginning of everything new. It resulted in new life to Jesus in His resurrection, new life to us in salvation, and many other new things as we live for Him.

In the same way, your suffering is for a purpose. While you may not see God's purpose, nor His will, you understand what God is doing in your life. You must believe that God has something for you on the other side of your suffering. It may be His anointing on your ministry in this life, or it may be preparation for your new life with Him in Heaven.

Complaining about your pain or suffering will only make you feel worse. When you spend your time focusing on your pain, remember that your focus consumes all of your thinking and controls your emotions. Your pain will flood your dreams and cancel your future positive dreams of doing things for God. So, when you constantly think about pain, the only thing on your mind is your suffering. However, think about Jesus; think about the Father's purpose in your life; think about how God is preparing you for future service and usefulness; think about becoming like Jesus Christ.

The joy of doing right can bring more relief from pain than wallowing in self-pity and constantly complaining. As pointed out earlier, wallowing in pain only makes your pain greater. The more you focus on your suffering, the more it controls your vision. Your suffering is the only thing you remember that caused your pain. But when you focus on doing right, and fulfilling the will of God, and pleasing Him, that will give you more relief from your pain than any thoughts about the cause of your suffering.

The solution to suffering is more than a positive mental attitude. There is an old saying when difficulties, pain, or problems come: "mind over matter." If you don't mind, it doesn't matter. Remember, God has promised, "He will not allow you to suffer more than you can bear" (1 Corinthians 10:13, ELT). And again Paul points our thinking to the LORD: "Let every detail of your life—words, actions, whatever—be done in the name of the Master—Jesus—thank God the Father for every step of the way" (Colossians 3:17, MSG).

Remember, God is in control. Yes, God is always in control, whether you recognize it or not: "God causes everything to work together for the good of those who love God and are called according to his purpose for them" (Romans 8:28, NLT). Whether you yield to Him or not, God is in control. When pain and suffering come, God can use it to strengthen you; or it can prepare you or mold you into His image. But even when you fight against God, He is still in control. The pain will continue and you will become more bitter ... more defeated ... and you can even destroy yourself because of pain.

So yield control of your life to Christ. Even yield your pain to Christ. When you are feeling well, your testimony is, "for me to live is Christ and to die is gain" (Philippians 1:21). We always quote the first part of that verse, but we neglect the last part: "to die is gain." So, when suffering comes, it may be the beginning of death. So recognize who controls your life, and yield control to Jesus Christ.

Never forget that you are never alone. God is with you in suffering as well as in triumphant moments. God is with you when you overcome sin and when you suffer. God is with you in those anointed moments when He uses you to share the Word of God or to give your testimony to another person.

Remember God's encouragement to Hosea: "Come, let us return to the Lord. He has torn us to pieces; now He will heal us. He has injured us; now He will bandage our wounds. In just a short time He will restore us, so that we may live in His presence. Oh, that we might know the Lord! Let us press on to know Him. He will respond to us as surely as the arrival of dawn or the coming of rains in early spring" (Hosea 6:1-3).

This same providence of God that allowed you to be afflicted and suffer is the same providence that can relieve and comfort you. Remember, God knows all things; He knows you and loves you. Also remember that God has control of all things, so He knows what you are suffering and why; God has a purpose for your suffering. But also remember that God has the power to do whatever He wants. So, when pain comes, God knows and God has a plan for your life. So find out what God wants you to do, and do it. Trust God: "'For I know the plans I have for you,' says the Lord. 'They are plans for good and not for disaster, to give you a future and a hope'" (Jeremiah 29:11).

Since God has a plan for your life, find it and follow it. And since God loves you, stand under His love and let Him shower you with His goodness. And since God has all power to do what He wants to do, find His presence, and live in it.

Chapter 2

HOW TO RESPOND TO SUFFERING AND PAIN

When you are happy, so happy, you have no sense
of needing Him [God], so happy you are tempted
to feel His claim upon you as an interruption ...
go to Him when your need is desperate, and when
other help is made, and what will you find? A door
slammed in your face, a sound of bolting and double
bolting on the inside. We don't always know why
suffering occurs, and, as Shepherd of the sheep, it is
our responsibility to show compassion and patience
at all times, especially the difficult ones. There
are no easy answers, sometimes questioning God's
whereabouts is a very human response. It shows how
desperately we are in need of His mercy and grace.

C. S. Lewis, *A Grief Observed*

WHAT is the most obvious reaction to pain? "It hurts!" And what is the next reaction to pain? "Stop! Go away!" And what is the next response to pain? "Why me? Why this? Why now?" But what is our ongoing reaction to pain? We begin to question the Almighty Himself: *Why are You doing this, God? Why is this pain so intense? Why now?*

There are various definitions of pain found in the different versions of Webster's Dictionary: (1) "Localized physical suffering associated with bodily disorder or disease or injury"; (2) "Basic bodily sensation, induced by noxious stimulus, received by naked nerve endings, characterized by physical discomfort and typically leading to evasive actions." Let's analyze the various definitions of pain from several points of view.

KINDS OF PAIN

1. Physical pain

There are all kinds of physical pain. If you accidentally stick yourself with a pin, it hurts. If you fall down some stairs, it hurts more in different places and in different ways. If you break a bone, it really hurts. If you are in an automobile accident and your head smashes the windshield, and you are knocked unconscious, it won't hurt at the time, but when you wake up, the pain will be agonizing.

The Bible tells a story of the Philistines attacking Israel, defeating their army, and capturing the Ark of God. Perhaps they lost the Ark of God because they were using it as a fetish, and their hope of defense was in the physical Ark of God and not in God Himself. The message of the defeat of Israel got back to the camp, and a woman there, "Eli's daughter-in-law, the wife of Phinehas, was pregnant and near her time of delivery. When she heard that the Ark of God had been captured, and that her father-in-law and husband were dead; she went into labor and gave birth. She died in childbirth" (1 Samuel 4:19-20). Before she died she named the child Ichabod, "the glory has departed." Notice the different levels of intensity of her pain that led to her death: first, the pains of giving birth to a child; second, the news that her father-in-law and husband had died; and third, that the very presence of God in Israel (the Ark of the Covenant) had been captured by the enemy.

2. Mental pain

Sometimes physical pain causes mental pain, but not always. Some mental pain has no connection to the physical. There can be painful thoughts that we don't want to face, but they destroy our dreams, our self-identity, even our future. The psalmist cried out, "When I thought to know this, it was too painful for me" (Psalm 73:16, KJV).

3. Inter-relationship pain

Sometimes our physical pain causes worry, fear, grief, and anguish. So you have physical hurt, but you also hurt mentally and emotionally. Then other times your mental and emotional pain are because you may have lost money, a goal that you cherished, or a prized object. That loss causes pain in the soul. That may or may not lead to physical pain. But on many occasions mental and emotional pain lead to all types of physical reactions, e.g., headaches, nausea, and even sickness.

4. The pain of losing someone in death

At the introduction of this chapter the story of C. S. Lewis describes his pain when he lost his wife. I understand C. S. Lewis's pain, because I remember when I lost my wife on December 13, 2013. My life and ministry were wrapped up in my wife, Ruth. We did many things together; we ministered together, prayed together, and dreamed together. But those were all gone. No one can measure the pain of another's loss in death, and it is difficult to comfort them other than being there with them and praying with them.

PHYSICAL PAIN

1. Acute pain

Acute pain is usually short term and easily identifiable for its cause. You immediately recognize this pain by its effect on you. This type of pain can go away just as quickly as it comes, and you don't even think about it any longer. You may even forget about it, and life goes on as if you never had the pain.

2. Chronic pain

Chronic pain usually is a longer, more enduring pain than other pains. Sometimes it is a pain that has outlived its original purpose. While people may have a scar on their physical body, they sense an ongoing pain where the scar is located; even though the wound has healed, they still have physical reactions—not because of the original wound, but pain persists in the same location of the body. This type of pain has outlived the original wound and the body does not need physical healing, but the pain still persists.

3. Cutaneous pain

This a localized pain, usually an injury to the skin or the skin surface. The word "cutaneous" comes from the Latin *cutis*, which means "skin." So this is superficial pain to the body, which is usually localized to the skin. The pain does not come from within the body/muscles but is a localized surface pain.

4. Somatic Pain

This is an inner pain in the ligaments, blood vessels, or bones. This is usually a dull but persistent pain. Sometimes it is difficult to locate this pain because it is so generalized over a section of the body. But nevertheless, it causes pain.

5. Visceral Pain

This is pain from the body's viscera, or organs. Visceral pain is related to the internal organs in the midline of the body. Unlike somatic pain, which occurs in the skin's tissue, visceral pain is hard to identify because of its deep location, causing pressure. Visceral pain includes and is associated with a variety of disorders, such as gallstones, pancreatitis, acute appendicitis, diverticulitis, or pain in the bowels, such as dyspepsia.

6. Phantom Pain

This pain comes from a body part that is usually no longer there. Sometimes doctors consider this a post-amputation phenomenon that is a psychological problem. Now medical experts recognize that these are real sensations that can originate in the nervous system of the body, i.e., spinal cord or the brain. This pain can feel like burning, twisting, or aching, or a quick flash or zing. Pain may happen only once or twice, or it could be a continuous and repetitive pain. Even though this is primarily a psychological problem, people have found that over-the-counter pain relievers, such as Tylenol, aspirin, ibuprofen, etc., can relieve the phantom pain. Also, you may need physical or occupational therapy and/or general massaging of the area.

When you think in terms of phantom pain, also remember the phrase "phantom limb." This is a sensation that some people experience. The limb has been amputated but people still act, feel, and respond as though the limb was still attached to the body. The nervous system responds to move the phantom limb, such as reaching out with the hand that is no longer there, or using fingers that no longer exist.

7. Neuropathy pain

Neuropathy pain is often described as a shooting or burning pain. It can come and go, and sometimes it is chronic, returning many times. Because it is unrelenting and severe, sometimes it causes nerve damage or other malfunctions in the nervous system.

What can cure neuropathy pain? There are some pain treatments for neuropathic pain; some are over-the-counter, such as Aleve and Motrin, which can ease the pain. Others may require a stronger painkiller.

MENTAL PAIN

Because God created the physical body as a unit, it is an organic whole that operates both independently and interdependently at the same time. Pain in one area of the body can affect other areas of the body. Pain that is mental can affect the physical, and pain that is emotional can affect other parts of the body.

1. Pain because of physical death

This pain is illustrated by the story of David mourning over his son Absalom. First Absalom rebelled against David and fled to Geshur. The Bible says, "David mourned for his son many days" (2 Samuel 13:37). This was emotional pain. Absalom came back to his father and again rebelled. Absalom led a violent revolution that threw David out of Jerusalem. Absalom took over his throne and the kingdom. David and his loyal followers left Jerusalem, crossed the Jordan River, and went to live in the wilderness. Eventually there was a battle between the forces of Absalom and David. In the battle Absalom was killed. When word got back to King David that his son was dead, "The king was overcome with emotion ... and burst into tears ... he cried, 'O my son Absalom! My son, my son Absalom! If only I had died instead of you! O Absalom, my son, my son'" (2 Samuel 18:33, NLT). There was intense emotional pain when David lost fellowship with Absalom, but there was extreme emotional and physical pain when David lost Absalom to death.

2. Loss of dreams or plans

God had called His people out of Egypt. He delivered them from the bondage of tyranny and captivity in Egypt. He led them into the desert. Then triumphantly they marched through the Dead Sea, where Pharaoh's army was drowned. Then they started marching across the desert toward the Promised Land, but Israel sinned ... terribly. They made an idol and worshipped it instead of God. Then God announced that they could not go to the Promised Land. "When the people heard these stern words, they went into mourning" (Exodus 33:4). Imagine that all your dreams were lost. Israel's dream of the Promised Land was lost; all adults 20 years old and older died in the wilderness.

Some men when they lose a job also lose both their dreams and their livelihood, and they resort to alcohol and despair, giving up on life. Some women might have been great housekeepers, but after a divorce they go into lethargy, giving up on life. Their world comes crashing down.

What does it take to get over the loss of dreams? New dreams. What does it take to get over the loss of purpose in life? A new purpose in life. God always offers renewal ... revival. God says, "Return to Me and live."

3. Memory

Sometimes our memory can cause us more pain than our physical body. We remember what we lost, and we remember former days. This is more than daydreaming, and this is more than living in the past. This is described as grief and suffering because we remember what we no longer have. Nehemiah was the cupbearer to King Artaxerxes of Persia, who ruled over the Near East, including the Holy Land. Nehemiah heard how the city of Jerusalem was desolate, burned, the temple torn down. Then Nehemiah was told about the people there: "They are in great trouble and disgrace. The wall of Jerusalem has been torn down, and gates have been destroyed by fire" (Nehemiah 1:3). His reaction was grief. "When I heard this, I sat down and wept. In fact, for days I mourned" (Nehemiah 1:4). Nehemiah was weeping and mourning over a place he had never visited and over a city where he had never lived; he had always lived in luxury in the king's palace, serving the king. But his memory of the Lord his God, and what He had done for the people in the past, caused him great grief. Perhaps his greatest motivation was the destruction of God's temple.

4. Conviction of sin

When God convicts us of sin, what does He do? He opens our spiritual eyes so that we see our sin, what it has done to us, and how it has destroyed our relationship with God. The word "convict" means "to cause to see." When you are convicted, you see your sin. Jesus said of the Holy Spirit, "When He comes, He will convict (to cause to see) the world. He will cause you to see the influence of sin in your life, of how you have lost God's presence and of your coming judgment" (John 16:7-8, ELT).

James tells us that when we see our sin, we will mourn because of painful memories that God brings to our mind. We will even weep, which is an outward display of our inner hurt. "Be afflicted, and mourn, and weep" (James 4:9, KJV).

5. Repentance of sin

Zechariah describes the pain Israel suffered in the presence of God. Israel went into the presence of the Lord to fast during the days of Yom Kippur. They would fast to seek His presence. Then in the presence of God they saw their sin as never before. Zechariah writes, "During these seventy years of exile, when you fasted and mourned" (Zechariah 7:5). So here Israel was in exile and they suffered the pain of memory and mourned because of everything they had lost in the Holy Land. They remembered what God had done for them in the past, so they mourned over their sin that caused their loss. Now in the presence of God, it brought them pain.

6. Over loss of life

God gives us a picture of people mourning; because of their sin, they are losing their life. Their pain and suffering are not due to physical suffering but because they are dying. "At the end you will groan in anguish when the disease consumes your body" (Proverbs 5:11).

7. Deprivation

Sometimes we deprive ourselves of things that we need, such as when we fast and go without eating. As a result we suffer pain. Perhaps we deprive ourselves of sleep or some other physical necessity; as a result we suffer pain. In one sense, going through self-discipline with the view of having a better body involves pain. But God gives a picture of the joys of Heaven compared to our deprivation here on Earth: "Yet what we suffer now is nothing compared to the glory he will reveal to us later" (Romans 8:18).

8. Identificational pain

When someone in your family is suffering, you may identify with them and suffer with them. When you see them crying, you may not have actual tears in your eyes, but you hurt as much as they do. Paul describes this suffering in the body of Christ: "If one member suffers, all the members suffer" (1 Corinthians 12:26). All Christians are members of the body of Christ, and every local church is a picture of that body. If someone in our church suffers, we identify with their pain, and thus we suffer as they suffer. Because we feel their suffering and loss, we may contribute money to help them with their suffering, or we pray for them, or we console them. We may help them by sending flowers, cards, and making phone calls. It is identificational pain that moves us to action.

TRUTH ABOUT PAIN

What is pain? Pain is far more than a physical reaction to discomfort or an emergency in our body. Pain is a complex mixture of emotions, experiences, sensation, physical coordination, and mental focus. Pain raises your blood pressure, increases your heart and breathing rate, and causes muscle tension. All these things are hard on the body and can lead to fatigue, sleeping problems, loss of appetite, and a feeling of tiredness, or it can cause you to go to sleep.

Medical experts have determined that pain that lasts a long time can lower your life span. Chronic pain, such as arthritis, back pain, recurring migraines, if left untreated, can also shorten a person's life.

People dealing with long-term or ongoing pain may become irritable, impatient, short-tempered, and suffer many other pains. Pain lowers the threshold of good health and creates problems for basic physical functioning of the body. As a result, many people with pain have difficulty finding solutions for their pain, and sometimes they don't even seek a relatively mundane solution to their problem.

Recent studies have shown that chronic pain can actually affect the brain's chemistry. That happens in the wiring of the nervous system. As a result of chronic pain, sections of the brain connected to the spinal cord and the nervous system of the body produce depression, or shut down normal physical reactions.

The more physical pain a person endures, the more difficult it is for that person to deal with multiple things at the same time. They may be able to do one or two things at the same time, but they can't do multiple things as they did previously. They also have problems focusing. A person with pain usually focuses on his pain. When forced to think about something else, he can think about a few things, but it is more difficult for the person to think creatively, to think positively, and to think of times when they were healthy. Pain influences visions, dreams, and plans for the future.

1. Pain as punishment.

When Adam and Eve sinned in the garden, it was the woman who first took the fruit and ate, giving it to Adam. Her punishment was tied to pain in childbearing. God said, "I will greatly multiply thy sorrow ... in sorrow thou shall bring forth children" (Genesis 3:16, KJV).

2. Pain is inevitable.

Because we are a physical body, we live within the limitations of that body. It will grow with excitement and possibilities until we reach a certain age. Then bodily functions begin to lose their effectiveness and die. Just as our skin dies on a regular basis and reproduces itself with new life, so too our body begins to reproduce itself with new life. But ultimately it is moving toward death and pain. Job recognized the inevitability of pain: "For affliction does not come from the dust, nor does trouble spring from the ground; yet man is born to trouble, as the sparks fly upward" (Job 5:6-7).

3. Pain corrects us to do right.

Many times when we get sick, God wants us to slow down, change our eating habits, change our sleeping habits, and do what is necessary to relieve the pain. In that sense, pain becomes our teacher. Our suffering from our pain forces us to change our life or way of doing things. "As a man chasteneth his son, so the Lord thy God chasteneth thee" (Deuteronomy 8:5, KJV). So, in this sense, God uses pain to be our teacher. Then God tells the benefits of why He punishes: "Behold, happy is the man whom God corrects; therefore do not despise the chastening of the Almighty" (Job 5:17).

4. Pain is one of God's ministries.

Job went through many types of suffering: he lost his children, home, crops, staff, everything. Yet Job understood God was working in his life: "The Lord gives and the Lord takes away. May the name of the Lord be blessed" (Job 1:21, ELT). Then Job said, "When He tests me, I will come out as pure as gold" (Job 23:10). Job knew, even though he was suffering, that God would reward him. "So the Lord blessed Job in the second half of his life even more than in the beginning" (Job 42:12). The Bible goes on to describe his larger crops, flocks, and more children compared to the his life before suffering (see Job 42:10-13).

5. God will help us in our pain.

Yes, God knows you are going to have pain in a world of suffering and affliction. God knows you will have difficulties and trials. So He promises that He will be with you. Claim the promise of the Shepherd's psalm: "Yea, though I walk through the valley of the shadow of death, I will fear no evil; for You are with me" (Psalm 23:4).

Fear not, for I am with you; be not dismayed, for I am your God. I will strengthen you, yes, I will help you, I will uphold you with My righteous right hand. (Isaiah 41:10)

6. We must all endure suffering.

As I went through many colleges and seminaries, I had many wonderful friends. I noticed that some seemed to have lots of money, while I had to work hard, and that led to other difficulties. What was God doing in our lives? Some had spiritual victory while others had spiritual problems I did not know about. Some had an easier time making A's because they did not have to study; others had difficulties, struggling with their studies. Paul realized that young Timothy was going to have difficulties and struggles. Paul's advice to Timothy also applies to us: "You therefore must endure hardship [suffer] as a good soldier of Jesus Christ" (2 Timothy 2:3).

7. You have a duty to the hurting.

Maybe right now you do not have suffering, nor any physical pain, or financial pressures, or other problems in life. But remember, you have a duty to those who are hurting. We are challenged, "Weep with those who weep" (Romans 12:15). Again, in the book of Hebrews we are told to "suffer with them who are suffering, share the sorrow of being mistreated, for you know what they are going through" (Hebrews 13:3, ELT).

8. Successful suffering leads to God's grace.

Paul understood suffering. As an apostle he wrote to the young church at Corinth to remind them of his sufferings and how God promised him victory: "My grace is sufficient for you, for My strength is made perfect in weakness. Therefore most gladly I will rather boast in my infirmities, that the power of Christ may rest upon me" (2 Corinthians 12:9). Notice that in suffering, Paul's imperfections were made perfect and his weakness was made strong. So what was Paul's reaction? "Most gladly therefore will I rather glory in my infirmities" (12:9). Is that your reaction?

ATTITUDES TO ASSUME IN SUFFERING

1. Since suffering is inevitable, don't think it is unusual.

Suffering, like birth and death, happens to all of us, because we were born into a life that includes both joys and sorrows, both pain and triumph. But you cannot call suffering a birth*right*. Actually the only "right" thing about suffering is what it can do for you, what it can make of you, and how it can mold your life and future. Not only does God use suffering for His glory, but He also uses it to conform us to be like Jesus Christ.

2. Don't immediately think God is punishing you for a particular sin.

Too often we have guilty consciences. When we begin to suffer, we begin to examine our conscience, asking, "What did it do wrong?" It all begins when we say, "Why, God?" or "Why me?" Don't question God when suffering comes; ask yourself, "Why not?" If God wants you to be more holy, He may allow more suffering in your life for many purposes. He may want to draw you closer to Himself. He may want to prune out some bad habits, or sin. He may allow suffering in your life as a positive teaching experience. If God wants to use you greatly in ministry, again He may allow you to suffer.

3. Pain protects, because the body shuts down when facing danger and damage.

God gives us pain to protect us. Think of when you touch something hot. You jump back in pain. But that reaction prevents you from getting worse burns. Your pain could keep you from even more dangerous results, or even death. Remember the last time you broke a bone, how it throbbed as you yelled for relief? Actually the pain was telling you to not use that limb, e.g., foot, hand, or arm. If you don't give that limb time to heal, you can do more damage.

Remember, the mind is a powerful tool. It can make us do many good things. Out of our mind come visions of what we could do. Thinking is the first step toward planning, and the next step is movement to accomplish our plans. Sometimes God uses pain to activate our mind to accomplish His purpose of healing us.

Technically pain is one function of the brain or the mind. Pain occurs when our brain activates an alarm signal of danger that needs our attention. Yes, some physical injuries activate a pain signal that may keep us from further physical injuries.

Actually, pain is a message our brain is sending us to do something about a physical injury or threat. Technically the message does not come to us in English. It's an immediate physical/nervous/mental response of alarm. The mind/body receives the message and applies the message so that we make the correction or application. If you break an ankle, your brain tells you to stop walking on that foot.

Of course, not all pain ends up in a message. Our brains *choose* what kind of message it will give us at any particular time about any particular injury. However, pain will have a message of some kind, whether related to our physical, emotional, psychological, or even spiritual facilities.

4. Some suffering is tied to sin.

Remember the man whom Jesus healed on His way to the temple? As Jesus approached the Pool of Bethesda, He saw a great multitude of sick, lame, blind, and feeble people. They were waiting for the stirring of the water so they could jump in and get healed. But there was one man who could not get into the water. There was no one to help him. He had been there 38 years. Something had happened to his legs so he could no longer walk. Jesus healed him and said, "Rise, take up your bed and walk" (John 5:8). The man was healed and went leaping and dancing into the temple to worship God. Jesus found him later in the temple and said, "See, you have been made well. Sin no more, lest a worse thing come upon you" (John 5:14). He had committed some sin that caused his suffering. If he went back into the same sin, there would be even more intense suffering.

5. Remember Christ's suffering.

Peter reminds us that we were called to suffer: "For to this you were called, because Christ also suffered for us, leaving us an example, that you should follow His steps" (1 Peter 2:21). Because Christ suffered for us, Peter told us that we are called to suffer with Him and for Him.

6. Don't be ashamed if you suffer because of your faith.

Peter tells us, "If anyone suffers as a Christian, let him not be ashamed, but let him glorify God in this matter" (1 Peter 4:16). The phrase "not be ashamed" means don't try to hide our suffering or to excuse it. However, we should not glorify our suffering, or make it a red badge of courage, i.e., a bragging point.

7. Learn from suffering and pain since it has a divine purpose.

Some people go through life angry at anything that holds them back, or slows down their growth, or ties their hands to keep them from doing what they want to do in life. However, God may have a purpose for the pain that has tied your hands. God may have a plan for your life that you don't see yet. So find God's plan and do it. If God has a purpose for your suffering, find out what it is, and suffer and glorify Him in all that you do.

8. Commit your soul to God when suffering.

Again Peter tells those who are suffering to make sure their relationship with God is strong: "Therefore let those who suffer according to the will of God commit their souls to Him in doing good, as to a faithful Creator" (1 Peter 4:19).

9. You probably will leave this life in pain.

If death comes in your sleep and you leave life without pain ... wonderful! If you have a stroke that instantly leads to death, look forward with anticipation. However, most people will leave this life with suffering and pain. The old body wears out, the eyes don't see as well, and the mind does not remember as well. The fingers are not as agile to do those fine little things we have done. Remember, the Bible speaks about the "pains of death" (Acts 2:24). The psalmist described the experience of death: "Death wrapped its ropes around me; the terrors of the grave overtook me. I saw only trouble and sorrow" (Psalm 116:3).

No one wants to die, but we are all going to meet God, and that is usually through some type of pain at death. However, you may be one of the few left behind to be raptured up to meet Christ in the air in the future. If so, rejoice in going to be with Jesus.

Chapter 3

WHEN PAIN HURTS

*If God were good, He would wish to make
His creatures perfectly happy, and if God were
almighty, He would be able to do what He
wished. But the creatures suffer pain; therefore,
does God lack goodness or power, or both?*

C. S. Lewis

THREE MYTHS ABOUT PAIN

FIRST, some believe you must not suffer pain because you are God's children. They think that God is great and powerful, and He can do whatever He wants. Since God is good and would not harm His children, they say we should not have any pain.

Second, if I hurt, there must be something wrong with me. This is not pain associated with a bruise or break or cut. No, some people feel they should never have pain and when they do there must be something wrong internally. When they suffer loss, they have pain. So, rather than seeking the physical cause of their pain, they immediately look within psychologically.

The third myth deals with people's wrong assumption of God. They say that if I hurt, there must be something wrong with God. Is this the person who usually blames their parents, friends, spouse, so now they blame God?

The answer to the three myths is that pain is a fact of life. When a baby is born, the doctor slaps the baby, inflicting pain, and the baby immediately cries. Then when you die, it is usually ushered in with the pain of death.

Therefore, pain is one explanation of life ... a fact of life ... and an answer to life ... and pain is inevitable.

WHY PAIN?

When God created Adam and Eve, He created them with a free will to do what they wanted to do. Did you notice that word, "free will"? How free was the will of Adam and Eve, and could they do anything they wanted to do ... anything outside the will of God ... anything that would displease God?

God gave to humans the power to do all that is intrinsically possible within the limits of His laws and the natural world. But man cannot do the impossible.

With that gift, man has the power to use his free will anyway he wants ... foolishly ... constructively ... to ruin his future, or to invest in the future. What does that mean? Man lives in a world of freedom that seems to be independent from God. Man can do anything he wants to do; he can please God or displease God. He can search for God or deny the existence of God.

Is this in keeping with the intent of an all-wise God? An all-powerful God? An all-loving God?

God decided not to correct every wrong independent action by the human when it happened. Because God gave humans their freedom, God decided to see if the man's/woman's independent nature would choose to love and follow Him. But God also wanted to see if they would choose to turn from God and reject Him.

It looks as though God gives humans what they want. If they want their freedom from Him, God lets them go that way. If they want their own way, God gives them that choice. It looks like God gives His people what they want, not what they need.

The human's free will included the possibility of evil, and men and women can become evil when they do evil. As a matter of fact, long before they do evil, they become evil when they desire evil ... think evil ... plan evil ... and begin acting in an evil way.

There is a problem when humans do evil. They think that time will cancel their evil deeds, or their sin—since they were not immediately punished every time they did evil. What goes on in man's mind? "I got away with it!"

That leads to a second thought. Man thinks that if everyone else is doing it, it is normal and alright for him to do it. But he thinks even further: since they do it and enjoy it and they get away with it—they are not punished—then it is alright for him to do it.

But life goes on and actions have consequences. Sometimes the consequences are immediate: You fall off of a rock and break an arm. You make a mistake with a knife and cut yourself. Or you don't watch where you are walking and you smash your foot. Some people say that is just life! Other people say that is stupid! Other people say you are irresponsible! And still other people say you should not have done that!

The human spirit will not surrender to God as long as everything is going well. But God uses pain as one tool to teach you something about life. Pain brings immediate consequences to your attention: you did something wrong and it hurts. Sometimes you don't realize you did something wrong until the pain comes; then you realize what you did was stupid.

Pain is a great teacher because it insists on getting your attention. If a broken finger is throbbing, it will continue hurting you until you do something about it.

Therefore, pain shatters the illusion of self-sufficiency. We think we can do what we want, but pain stops us. We think we can go where we want, but pain stops us. We think we can act any way, say anything, and go anywhere, but pain teaches us the limits of life.

The Bible teaches a positive element of pain. It suggests, "being made perfect through suffering" (Hebrews 2:10). Do we think our pain will make us better? Will our pain make us avoid the thing that hurts us in the future? Do we think our pain will produce a higher quality of life? Probably not!

PAIN IS NOT GOOD IN ITSELF BUT A TOOL USED BY GOD

God's wonderful plan of Heaven does not include pain. "I John saw the holy city ... God shall wipe away all tears from their eyes ... there shall be no more death ... no sorrow ... no crying ... there shall be no more pain" (Revelation 21:4).

So what can you look forward to after you die in pain and you live with God in Heaven? Remember what Paul said: "For I consider that the sufferings of this present time are not worthy to be compared with the glory which shall be revealed in us" (Romans 8:18). And what does that mean? It does not mean that just because you suffer a lot on Earth, you will get a lot of joy in Heaven. The opposite is also not true, that if you suffer a little, you will only get a little joy in Heaven. Paul is saying you cannot compare your sufferings today to the joys you will have with God in glory.

HOW TO RESPOND IN PAIN

1. Accept what you cannot change.

Sometimes you go through suffering and you don't know what to do. All you can do is accept your pain. There comes a time when a pill to take away the pain is not enough, nor is a nap in the afternoon enough to make you forget. Sometimes you just have to accept your pain and suffering in the situation where you find yourself.

David committed the sin of adultery with Bathsheba, not his wife. She got pregnant and had David's child out of wedlock. It was embarrassing because David was a man of God, and it was more embarrassing because all the children of the king were in line for the throne. But even more than that, David went through agony of the conviction of his sin, and the child became sick unto death. So, David prayed ... fasted ... and agonized for his little boy who was born to him and Bathsheba. When the child died, David got up from the ground and said, "While the child was still alive, I fasted and wept ... but now that he is dead, why should I fast?" (2 Samuel 12:22-23).

David could do nothing about the death of the child. He could do nothing about his reputation. All he could do was get up and accept the consequences and go about his life. In the same way, you must accept what you cannot change.

2. Don't exaggerate your pain.

Some people want to ignore their pain, or sometimes they exaggerate it far beyond its intensity. They play it up or pray it down. What did David do? After the baby died, "he went into the house of the LORD and worshiped" (2 Samuel 12:20). You must forget your pain and go on with your life. And like David, you worship God with all your heart.

3. Focus on the good you have left of life.

When you have gone through pain, don't focus on the bad or the pain of your past. Even if your pain was intense but is now gone, don't focus on it ... remember it ... and rejoice that it is gone. No, focus on the good health and good life you have left. So what did David do after he left his time of prayer and fasting? He left the house of the Lord where he worshipped God and then "David comforted his wife ... she gave birth to a son and they named him Solomon" (2 Samuel 12:24).

So David realized he still had a wife, even though they sinned together before he married her. So what did he do? He looked to the future. They had a second son, Solomon, who was the heir apparent to David's throne. Solomon would be the next king of Israel.

4. People may hurt you, but God replaces grudges with blessings.

Many people may dislike you because of what you have done, or they may hold a grudge against you, or try to retaliate. But Jesus said, "Bless them that curse you ... and pray for them which despitefully use you" (Matthew 5:44). In life you could take the *bitter* road when some people hurt you, or you could take the *better* road. What is the difference between *bitter* and *better*? One letter: "i." You are the "I" who can choose how to react in every situation.

If I allow pain to make me bitter, it blinds me to the truth of what God wants for my life. (Martin Luther)

5. Let God do His job.

You don't live in Heaven, where there is no pain, suffering, or mistakes. This is earth, where God allows pain, and He uses it for the purpose of keeping you from further harm, or to make your life better, and sometimes to save your life from death. In Heaven all wrongs are made right, and all pain is eliminated and you live happy forever more.

You live on this earth where pain is a *given*. Pain—all types of pain will happen in this life. Pain—all types of pain will continually happen. Pain—all types of pain will come and go between the good days and the bad days. Since pain is written on the pages of every life here on Earth, let pain do its job, but more importantly let God do His job of relieving your pain.

6. Jesus wants to heal your hurting heart.

Jesus lived a perfect life without sin, but there were times when He suffered pain. Jesus was disappointed with the rich young ruler who did not respond to Him, but instead the rich young ruler walked away (see Matthew 19:24). Was Jesus's disappointment painful?

Also, when Jesus heard that his friend Lazarus had died, the Bible says, "Jesus wept" (John 11:35). As Jesus visited Lazarus's tomb, no one expected Him to raise the dead. Did those tears represent the pain of losing a friend, or pain because of the multitudes' unbelief?

7. Look past your pain.

In June 2003, my medical doctor did a colonoscopy on me and told me I had a small cancerous growth in my colon, the upper colon. I met him at the hospital and he was going to operate on me with a small one- or two-inch incision, and I would be an outpatient, perhaps going home that evening or the next morning. When the doctor got inside, the cancer was much larger than anticipated and he could not get it out with a one-inch incision. How big was the cut? About 13 inches long. That night in the hospital I hurt so much I thought I was going to die.

My pastor, Jerry Falwell, came to see me, and I will never forget his encouraging words: "Elmer, this pain will be a bad dream next week." I thought to myself, *Jerry, that is easy for you to say, but I am the one who is hurting.*

Now let me explain my pain. The hospital's night nursing staff had not been told to give me any sedative to relieve my pain. Around every 15 minutes I hurt so bad I prayed to die, but I did not. Then I would make the same prayer again the next 15 minutes. After 2 to 3 hours of pain, the nurse finally contacted the doctor and I was given pain medication and slept soundly the rest of the night.

The next morning I remembered why Jerry Falwell had told me, "Elmer, this pain will be a bad dream next week." So, yes, within a week the pain was completely gone. Much of the pain you go through now or in the future, after it is over, will just be a bad dream.

Chapter 4

WHY GOD
ALLOWS PAIN

GOD created a perfect man and woman and put them together in harmony. Then He placed them in a perfect environment in the Garden of Eden. Then the Lord met with them to fellowship with them each evening as they worshipped Him.

But then the woman ate the forbidden fruit, and the man followed her example. They both disobeyed God and sinned. "Wherefore, as by one man sin entered into the world, and death by sin; and so death passed upon all men, for that all have sinned" (Romans 5:12, KJV).

BUT WHAT IS THE QUESTION?

Some people ask the question, why do bad things happen to good people? They ask that question because they know some good people who had bad experiences.

But here's another question: why do good people do bad things? There are some leaders in the church who will break the law. There are ministers who will do bad things. There has always been a Peter who denied the Lord, and a Samson who gave into the evil temptations of a Delilah.

But the real question is, why do good people suffer pain and injury?

PAIN AND SUFFERING ARE THE CONSEQUENCES OF DISOBEYING GOD

God created the perfect world for Adam and Eve, and everything was provided for them. There was no pressure ... no failure ... no agony ... and no bad dreams. But Adam and Eve sinned.

"To the woman He said: 'I will greatly multiply your sorrow and your conception; in pain you shall bring forth children; your desire shall be for your husband, and he shall rule over you.' Then to Adam He said, 'Because you have heeded the voice of your wife, and have eaten from the tree of which I commanded you, saying, "You shall not eat of it": Cursed is the ground for your sake; in toil you shall eat of it all the days of your life. Both thorns and thistles it shall bring forth for you, and you shall eat the herb of the field. In the sweat of your face you shall eat bread till you return to the ground, for out of it you were taken; for dust you are, and to dust you shall return"' (Genesis 3:16-19). Because of the sin of Adam and Eve, sin entered the world, and with it pain and suffering.

GOD'S ULTIMATE PURPOSE

God has a purpose for you and for your life. What is God's intent? "'For I know the plans I have for you,' says the Lord. 'They are plans for good and not for disaster, to give you a future and a hope'" (Jeremiah 29:11, NLT).

God has an ultimate purpose for everyone and parts of that purpose are for them to be like Jesus: "For whom He foreknew, He also predestined to be conformed to the image of His Son" (Romans 8:29). Remember, God did not create you just to be happy or just to have a comfortable life. Also, God did not create you just to live pain free. Rather, God tells you, "I know the plans I have for you" (Jeremiah 29:11).

GOD SOVEREIGNLY USES PAIN
TO FULFILL HIS PURPOSE

God whispers in our pleasures, speaks in our conscience, but shouts in our pain. (C. S. Lewis)

1. Pain is for your protection.

What does pain do? It gets your attention and it keeps reminding you through suffering and agony. Because pain is usually constant, and sometimes gets worse, if you don't attend to it, it will cause serious problems. God gives you pain to keep you from further damage or more suffering.

Pain will constantly annoy you, but again, why? Pain is there to get your attention, because it wants to protect you from a disease perhaps, or maybe an unseen tragedy that the eye cannot see and the mind cannot conceive.

2. Pain can protect you from yourself.

The human personality, along with the physical body, usually thinks it is unstoppable ... and ongoing. But physical pain shouts, "*Stop!*"

Notice what Paul said about his constant pain: "And lest I should be exalted above measure ... there was given to me a thorn in the flesh, a messenger of Satan to buffet me, lest I should be exalted above measure" (2 Corinthians 12:7, KJV). We don't know what Paul's thorn in the flesh was. Some people think it was a disease of the eye that irritated him constantly. Other people think it was a speech problem, perhaps a stuttering, or some other difficulty with speech (that is why Paul said he did not speak with eloquent words). Still others think his thorn in the flesh was a physical problem of the skin and/or muscles. Whatever it was, Paul lived with it the rest of his life.

3. Pain can strengthen your character.

Pain hurts, and no one likes pain. But we learn to deal with it, and we manage it, and we overcome our pain or ignore it to carry out our work and do what is expected of us. Look at what James said about pain: "Dear brothers, is your life full of difficulties and temptations? Then be happy, for when the way is rough, your patience has a chance to grow. So let it grow, and don't try to squirm out of your problems. For when your patience is finally in full bloom, then you will be ready for anything, strong in character, full and complete" (James 1:2-4, TLB). So let your difficulties, or your pain, or your problems strengthen your inner person to go on serving the Lord.

4. Pain can strengthen your faith.

Your life is a walk of faith, and faith is looking to Jesus, realizing your relationship with Christ is the most important thing in life. While pain may try to be dampen your enthusiasm for Christ, or even stop you from serving the Lord altogether, you can overcome your pain. You serve Christ anyway. When you do that, you strengthen your faith and become a stronger Christian.

5. Pain prepares you to serve Christ better.

Joseph was the great-grandson of Abraham and a leader in the line of faith reaching back to Abraham. While Joseph did not do his primary work with the children of Abraham and his extended family, God used Joseph in Egypt to feed the world when a famine came. Because of what Joseph had learned from his suffering—wrongful imprisonments, lies, and rejections—he developed inner strength and character to serve God better. At the end of his life, when he looked at his 10 brothers, who were the ones who had caused his pain and suffering, Joseph said to his brothers, "You meant evil against me; *but* God meant it for good" (Genesis 50:20).

6. Pain draws you closer to Christ.

If you are like most people, when pain hits you, you immediately pray to God for relief. Then you ask God to help you get through the pain, and perhaps at times you pray asking God to keep you from dying. Paul went through much suffering as he served Jesus Christ. Through his sufferings Paul came closer to Christ and said, "...that I may know Him and the power of His resurrection, and the fellowship of His suffering, being conformed to His death" (Philippians 3:10). In this verse Paul identifies his sufferings with those of Jesus Christ.

7. Pain strengthen you to your life's purpose.

Think about it! When distractions try to keep you from finishing a task, you resolve to do it. So, when pain becomes a distraction, resolve even more to finish the task God has given you in life. So pain can strengthen your life's purpose. Remember what Paul said: "Therefore, I take pleasure in infirmities, and reproaches, in needs, in persecutions, in distress for Christ's sake. For when I am weak, then I am strong" (2 Corinthians 12:10).

8. Pain motivates you to action.

Think about a man who should go to the dentist to have his teeth cleaned once a year. That also involves letting the dentist examine all his teeth. But he puts it off, and before you know it, it is six months, nine months. And then after two and half years, he gets a terrible toothache. The pain of his toothache makes him go see the dentist. Whether he wants to admit it or not, his pain motived him to action. It was not his desire for good looks, sweet-smelling breath, or even clean teeth. No, his pain moved him to action.

9. Pain guides and teaches you.

It could be the pain of memory, when we realize that we forgot ... we failed ... we messed up. This could be the pain of a broken relationship: you did not show up ... you forgot the anniversary. It could be the pain of any type of trouble that causes discomfort or suffering. The psalmist said, "My troubles turned out all for the best—they forced me to learn from Your textbook" (Psalm 119:71, MSG).

10. Pain may protect you from a worse situation.

You should treat a small cut on your finger. But you do nothing because the pain is slight. Then the cut begins to hurt, so you do something about it. Then you discover the cut is infected, and you could have serious problems, possibly even an amputation of the finger. The psalmist described the pain that brought him to action: "I was on the verge of collapse, facing constant pain" (Psalm 38:17, NLT). Then the psalmist called on the Lord for help: "Come quickly to help me, O Lord my savior" (v. 22).

PART ONE

FAITH
WALKING
through
SUFFERING & PAIN

DEVOTIONS

Day 1

PAIN STRENGTHENS YOUR CHARACTER

*My brethren, count it all joy when you fall
into various trials, knowing that the testing
of your faith produces patience. But let
patience have its perfect work, that you may
be perfect and complete, lacking nothing.*

James 1:2-4

NOTICE how James begins this passage: "brethren, *when* troubles come your way." He didn't say "*if* troubles come your way." James knew Scripture, and he knew life—James knew that every child of God *would* have troubles. Job said it best: "People are born for trouble as readily as sparks fly up from a fire" (Job 5:7). Everyone has troubles; either they just got through trouble, or they are in trouble now, or troubles will meet them soon. But don't live a negative life looking for trouble. No! Live a positive life. Consider problems an opportunity to grow in Christ. If you do that, it will change your perspective on life. Look through your problems to see God, and in every problem find a way to grow in grace and grow to be like Jesus.

*Lord, I don't like problems, but I will use them as a means
of growing to be like Jesus. Help me be ready for trials, help*

me see how to handle them, and give me grace and courage to live through all the suffering that comes my way. Amen.

James tells us that when troubles come, our faith will grow. How big is your faith? If it is not very big, perhaps you haven't learned from troubles how to solve them and how to grow because of them. One more thing about faith: remember, faith is your relationship with God. So He uses pain to strengthen your faith and your relationship with Him. Perhaps God has allowed trouble to give your faith possibility to grow.

Lord, I want to grow my faith; help me to grow without trouble. But since problems are everywhere, and I have them, use my problems to grow my faith. May I trust You ... follow You ... and serve You. Amen.

READ:

JAMES 1:1-26

Day 2

TRIALS AND SUFFERINGS

*These trials will show your faith is
genuine ... as fire purifies gold.*

1 Peter 1:7, NLT

TRIALS and sufferings accomplish several things in our life. First, they conform us to be like Jesus Christ. Peter tells us trials will purify us as it does gold; "it will bring you peace ... when Jesus Christ is revealed" (1 Peter 1:7). But trials also will grow/strengthen your faith. James tells us, when "your faith is tested ... grows" (James 1:3). But your suffering also gets the attention of Jesus. "Since He Himself was gone through suffering ... He is able to help us when we are tested" (Hebrews 2:17-18). So look beyond your suffering; God is purifying you and He is strengthening you. And beyond that, remember, you have the attention of Jesus. Because He went through suffering, He will help you through your pain.

> *Lord, forgive me for worrying about my pain. Help me see why I am suffering and help me learn what You are teaching me. And help me get through this pain. Amen.*

There are going to be all types of suffering on Earth, and some will suffer much more than you. Your present suffering is probably worse than what you have had to endure in the past, and there may be a few worse days in the future. But look beyond your pain; look beyond your circumstance. Look to Jesus and ask for His presence in your situation, and pray for strength to endure and a willing mind to learn.

> *Lord, I look beyond my pain—I look to You for help. I know You went through suffering, so help me through my pain. Give me strength to bear pain, but also give me healing and give me victory over circumstances to praise You at all times. Amen.*

READ:

1 Peter 4:1-19

Day 3

SPIRITUAL EYES

*These trials will show that your faith is genuine ...
tested as fire tests and purifies gold—though your
faith is far more precious than mere gold. So, when
your faith remains strong through many trials, it
will bring you much praise and glory and honor.*

1 Peter 1:7, NLT

*When troubles come your way ... you know your
faith is tested ... a chance to grow. So let it grow.*

James 1:2,4

WHY are Christians surprised when they suffer persecution or pain? True, Christianity is a dominant religion but it's not the primary religion in many countries of the world. True, the God of Christianity promises many benefits to His followers, but Christians may be persecuted or suffer pain. True, when debates over which religion is correct, Christianity has high marks of winning in the eyes of many judges. So why do Christians—followers of Jesus—suffer so much and so often? Because there is an eternal struggle between good and evil, between God and satan. Satan will use his limited power to attack and punish followers of Jesus Christ. Satan will turn the human sin nature (lust of the flesh, lust of eyes, and pride of life) against believers. Satan will use every advantage he possesses to destroy Christianity and individual followers of Christ.

> *Lord, open my spiritual eyes to see all the temptations and trials satan throws against me. Then open my understanding to know all Your forces of righteousness that I can use to defeat satan. Now give me spiritual strength to oppose satan ... temptation .. and sin. Jesus, I want You to be victorious in my life. Amen.*

Sometimes we get so focused on one small temptation—which seems large and threatening—that we lose sight of the indwelling Jesus who will protect us. We forget about the indwelling Holy Spirit, who will give us spiritual understanding, spiritual power, and spiritual victory. You are on God's side and He is on your side. By faith claim victory, and when it comes, give praise to the Father, Son, and Holy Spirit.

> *Lord, send the Holy Spirit to give me spiritual eyes to see and understand the spiritual battle around me. Send Jesus to show Himself strong in my defense. Father, come bring Your power into my life, and when I gain victory, You get the praise! Amen.*

READ:

1 Peter 1:1-25

Day 4

GOD'S PURPOSE FOR YOUR SUFFERING

For God called you to do good, even if it means
suffering, just as Christ suffered for you. He is
your example, and you must follow in his steps.
He never sinned, nor ever deceived anyone.

1 Peter 2:21-22, NLT

GOD has a purpose for your life. He wants to do good for you, and He wants to use you to do good for/to others. Notice what Peter added: "even if it means suffering" (v. 21). Most of us never think about the good we can do for God when we are suffering. Usually, we are so busy with our pain that we never think about others, or any good thing we could do. But Peter reminds us to do good even when we suffer. Why? Because we follow the example of Jesus, who went about doing good, even when He suffered. Sometimes we suffer because we do dumb things, or we don't take care of our bodies. Sometimes we suffer because bad things happen to us.

> *Lord, help me look beyond my suffering to remember the ex-*
> *ample of Jesus. Help me focus on others when I suffer, and*
> *help me do good to them. Also, heal me and make the pain*
> *go away. Amen.*

Yes, God has a purpose for your life. He wants to use you to help/bless others. So in your pain, pray for others in pain; do something good for those in need. Look beyond your circumstances. Others may have more pain/need than you. When you focus on other people, you sometimes forget about your pain, or you realize your pain is not as bad as their suffering. It is good to get your mind off yourself—even when you hurt—for someone else may have greater pain/need than you.

Lord, forgive me for thinking primarily of myself. Help me see others and understand their pain. Then guide me to help them, and when I do, make my pain go away. Amen.

READ:

1 Peter 2:1-22

Day 5

HELPING OTHERS

We live in such a way that no one will stumble because of us, and no one will find fault with our ministry. In everything we do, we show that we are true ministers of God. We patiently endure troubles and hardships and calamities of every kind. We have been beaten, been put in prison, faced angry mobs, worked to exhaustion, endured sleepless nights, and gone without food.

2 Corinthians 6:3-5, NLT

LEARN from your suffering so that you can help others who have pain and suffering. When you live through your pain, then you are a testimony to others in pain. Perhaps they will hear about you and become encouraged. But also, God may give you opportunities to share with some what God has done for you. If you remember the pain you thought was too much for you, but you got through it, then you can encourage those in pain. You can encourage them, instruct them, and inspire them. So think back to your previous pain. Did someone encourage you and help you make it through your pain? Then you can do for others what someone did for you.

Lord, forgive me for focusing only on my pain. Help me pray for others in suffering; then help me encourage them and help them make it through. Use me as a testimony. Amen.

When you are in the middle of pain, think about two previous experiences. First, remember a previous pain that made you feel almost as bad as you now suffer. Did you get through the pain that last time? Then you can get through it again. But also remember the good feeling when your pain was gone. You can have that good feeling in the future. So hope in God and pray for healing.

Lord, I thank You for getting me through my past pain—get me through this pain. I remember how good I felt when the past pain was gone—do it again. Amen.

READ:

2 Corinthians 6:1-18

Day 6

THE ATTITUDE OF JESUS CHRIST

Your attitude should be the same that Christ
Jesus had ... He did not demand or cling to
His rights ... He made Himself nothing ... in
human form He obediently humbled Himself
... by dying a criminal's death on a cross.

Philippians 2:5,7-8, ELT

TOO often we think we are too good to suffer, or we think it is not right for us to suffer, or we attack the person or thing that is making us suffer. We demand our rights! But look at Jesus's suffering. Isn't He our example? And aren't we to follow His steps (see 1 Peter 2:21)? Therefore let Jesus be your example and accept your suffering. Then determine to learn from your suffering so it won't happen again. But if your suffering is inevitable—because of circumstances or a physical sickness—then determine to glorify God by assuming the attitude of Jesus when He suffered. Then pray "not my will, but Thine be done."

Lord, all kinds of pain hurts—physical, emotional, and
psychological. Help me deal with pain as best I can, and if
possible, give me relief from pain. If no relief, help me make
it through. Amen.

Jesus suffered pain in His death. What else could He do? He yielded Himself to God as the sacrifice for my/your sins. He suffered for me so I won't have to suffer in hell. That is eternal relief. Now He can help you through your present pain.

> *Lord, when it hurts, I want to give up, but I cannot do that. When it gets worse, I will only cry to You. My trust is in You, and I will bear my pain, just as Jesus did. May I glorify You in all I do. Amen.*

READ:

Philippians 2:1-30

Day 7

WHEN PERSECUTION COMES

*If the world hates you, remember
that it hated me first.*

John 15:18, NLT

*Since they persecuted me, naturally
they will persecute you.*

John 15:20, NLT

THERE are many reasons why Christians are persecuted and suffer. Yes, we live in an evil world, and when we live righteously, sin will come after us. People in the world follow their evil desires, so they will not respect you when you live for God but will persecute you. Didn't Peter tell us there were evildoers (see 1 Peter 2:12)? Beyond that the world is driven by "the lust of the flesh, the lust of the eyes, and the pride of life" (1 John 2:16). So when Jesus warned us to expect persecution, why are we surprised when it comes? You need to ask God to give you "Jesus eyes" so you can see the wicked nature of society, and ask for a "Jesus mind" to understand why sin grinds on you.

Lord, give me Your eyes to understand society and human nature. Don't overwhelm me with the evil I see, but help me understand where my persecution is coming from. Then give me grace to accept it, Your power to endure it, and Your courage to correct what can be prevented. Amen.

Persecution of good things and good people is one of the facts of life. You will have to accept it but also understand the nature and source of evil that attack God's servants. Then you must guard against it, as you stiffen your resolve to stand against it. Then pray for strength to stand, but also pray for wisdom to deal with it or eliminate it.

Lord, You are my guide in life. Lead me through trouble and persecution. Help me make good decisions about all things, especially about trouble and persecution. Then, Lord, save me. Amen.

READ:

John 15:1-8; 16:6

Day 8

JESUS KNOWS JUST HOW MUCH

He will not allow you to suffer above
that you are able to bear.

1 Corinthians 10:13, ELT

WHEN you are suffering, realize God is in control. He knows you and loves you. He knows your pain, and you have His promise that He will not allow you to suffer more than you can stand. Yet, many have suffered tremendous pain and they think a particular pain has brought them to the end. Remember, Jesus suffered until He died. He understands your pain, and He will be with you. Even if the ultimate limit of your pain is death, He will be with you. Remember the promise David claimed: "Yea though I walk through the valley of the shadow of death ... Thou art with me" (Psalm 23:4, KJV).

Lord, I don't like pain. Be with me when I suffer and help
me make it through my agony. I will trust You in all things.
I trust You with my physical life and with my soul in death.
Amen.

The interesting thing about pain is, it makes us think about ourselves more than we usually do. It makes us think about what life was like before pain, and it makes us think/dream of life again without pain. So pain makes us think about the good days, but does it make you think about God ... and living with Him in Heaven ... and the joys of a life without pain?

> *Lord, I pray about my pain. Thank You for past days with good health and no pain. Now help me get through this pain. I pray for healing and wholeness. Please give me good health again. Amen.*

READ:

Job 42:1-17

Day 9

BECOMING A SOLDIER

You therefore must endure hardship as a good soldier of Jesus Christ. No one engaged in warfare entangles himself with the affairs of this life, that he may please him who enlisted him as a soldier.

2 Timothy 2:3-4

WHEN a young person enlists in the military, he/she is signing up for discipline, hardship, physical pain, and sacrifice. Think of all the things that will happen to a young person when they begin training for the military. There is physical pressure/ stress to make them physically stronger. There are demanding chores and jobs to make them resilient. There are parades and marches to make them obedient. All these pressures are to make a soldier tough, strong, obedient, and ready to fight. Isn't that what God does to us to equip us to serve Him ... defend Him ... fight against sin ... and win people to Jesus Christ? It is not easy being a first-class fighting soldier, and it is not easy being a first-class servant of God.

Lord, I want to be a first-class soldier in Your army and I want to serve You faithfully. I will go through all types of pressure to learn obedience and service. May I serve You to the best of my ability, and may it be profitable for Your glory. Amen.

There are many disciplines a young person must learn to be a first-class soldier. And there are just as many disciplines to acquire to be a first-class disciple of Jesus. Since Jesus wants the best, determine to be your best and give Him your best.

> *Lord, I will follow You to the best of my ability. Teach me all I need to know, make me all I have to become, and mold me into the person who will glorify You in life and in service. Amen.*

READ:

2 Timothy 2:1-26

Day 10

HELPING THOSE
WHO HURT

Weep with them that weep.

Romans 12:15

Suffer with them as though you were suffering,
share the sorrow of those being mistreated, for
you know what they are going through.

Hebrews 13:3, ELT

THE Bible teaches us that we have a duty to those who are hurting, whether they are suffering physical pain, psychological distress, or any other type of difficulty. We must weep with them, because we understand their pain, and we must pray for them. Pray they will learn from their suffering, they will make it through, and they will glorify Jesus in their suffering. Then beyond our spiritual identification, we must do all we can physically, financially, and mentally to help them in their suffering. They may not be able to help you in your suffering, but God has others who can/will help you in your pain.

Lord, give me a heart for those who are suffering, and lead me to help them when I can and how I can. I pray for their suffering and thank You that someday, someone will pray for me in my suffering. Amen.

When others are hurting, you may give physical or financial help. At other times you will be called upon to give emotional or psychological support. Then always you can give spiritual support—first, by praying for them, perhaps praying with others for them. Then maybe you can actually pray with them in their hour of need. What you do for others, God may send even another person to pray with you in your time of need.

Lord, give me a heart for hurting people. Remind me of those who helped me when I needed them. Thank You for friends in deed who have been there for me in my time of need. Amen.

READ:

Romans 12:9-21

HOW GOD USES PAIN

*You should know in your heart that as a man
chastens his son, so the Lord your God chastens you.*

Deuteronomy 8:5

*Behold, happy is the man whom God
corrects; Therefore do not despise the
chastening of the Almighty.*

Job 5:17

GOD uses pain as a teaching instrument. Doesn't a teacher motivate pupils to learn by using a chalkboard, films, books, etc.? But teachers also give tests or assignments with standards that stretch their pupils. The student who knows the answers passes the test, and those who are not prepared might fail. So life is like a classroom, where God our teacher is using many resources to teach us the lessons of life. God also gives tests or exams. Some pass with flying colors, and some fail. God puts us on Earth to learn, so there are tests to measure what we've learned. Failing a test is hard on the ego, and the child can be denied certain privileges at home. There is also punishment. The child may hurt mentally, psychologically, or physically when he/she doesn't pass a test.

Lord, help me learn the lessons of life quickly and easily so I don't have to suffer. But when I fail, help me repent and learn; then help me do right. Lord, life is a school; help me pass. Amen.

There are all types of pain in life. Sometimes we fail the lessons God is teaching us and we hurt financially, or emotionally, or we lose face among friends and family. Because there are so many facets to life, God teaches us in many different ways. But God also uses many types of pain to teach us before failure and/or after failure. Remember, one of God's purposes for us is to learn, and pain is one of the tools to help learning take place.

God, I don't like pain now, and I have never liked it in the past. Help me learn so I don't have to go through pain; then help me in pain to learn what You need to teach me. And when I am in pain, help me make it through. Amen.

READ:

Job 5:1-27

Day 12

LEARNING THROUGH SUFFERING

When He has tested me, I shall come forth as gold.

Job 23:10

GOD uses pain to make you better. Look at Job, a rich man who lost all his wealth. His children were killed, and he ended up in physical pain, yet in his physical misery, Job understood God was putting him through the fire. How could Job accept his suffering and praise God in the midst of suffering? Because Job's faith was in God. "In all this, Job did not sin, nor charge God with wrong" (Job 1:22). So what is your attitude toward pain? Do you blame someone at work, or your family, or your circumstances? Let's pause to look at suffering and try to see how God is using our pain to teach us something. Maybe you are not in pain now but you have been in the past, and it will come back in the future.

> *Lord, I don't like pain, but thank You for all the ways in the past that pain told me I needed medical help/discipline/relief. Help me see my pain through Your eyes, and help me learn from it to be a better, stronger person. Amen.*

When Job came through his suffering, God had purified him as pure gold—more valuable than ever before. Look beyond your pain. What will you learn from it? And how will you live better after your suffering is gone? Look at pain as a tempering tool to learn life's lessons. No one likes term papers, quizzes, or final exams. In the same way, no one likes pain and suffering. What can God teach you through a painful experience?

> *Lord, I don't like pain, and I don't even want to think about it. But it is a necessary tool to teach me the lessons of life. Give me inquisitive eyes to understand my pain, and give me a learning heart to grow from my pain. Amen.*

READ:

Job 23:1-23

Day 13

PAIN IS INEVITABLE

*I will greatly multiply your sorrow ... in
pain you shall bring forth children.*

Genesis 3:16

SOME things in life are inevitable—taxes must be paid; tires on cars wear out—and pain is part of life. When Adam and Eve sinned, they opened the door of pain to the world. If you fall, you will be hurt, or could kill yourself. When a woman gives birth to a baby, there will be labor pains. Some women seem to suffer more than others. Even with modern medication and pain remedies, still all pain cannot be blocked out. Pain is part of the fabric of life. So learn how to get around it when possible, how to endure it when inevitable, and how to subdue it with medication or a procedure when possible. The moment a baby is born, it cries, and when you leave this life in death, usually there is pain.

*Lord, help me be realistic about pain. Help me control it
with medication or other means when possible. Help me face
it as an experience of life, and teach me through suffering.
Help me overcome the fear of pain, and make me victorious
over it. Amen.*

Think about this: if there were no pain, you might do something harmful or even dangerous and kill yourself. But pain can save your life.

If there were no pain, we would not go see a doctor, or take medicine, or follow healthful precautions. Pain may have saved your life in many ways, but you don't realize it. So, before you curse your pain, thank God that it is part of life. Without pain you might be dead.

> *Lord, thank You for pain. Help me listen to it and learn from it. Help me find healing, and if not, help me endure it and learn from it. Then help me live better because of it. Amen.*

READ:

Revelation 21:1-7

Day 14

PRAYING ABOUT PAIN

Concerning this thing I pleaded with the Lord three times that it might depart from me. And He said to me, "My grace is sufficient for you, for My strength is made perfect in weakness." Therefore most gladly I will rather boast in my infirmities, that the power of Christ may rest upon me.

2 Corinthians 12:8-9

IN today's verse, Paul is praying about his pain. He called it a "thorn in the flesh." We don't know what it was, but some think it was an eye irritation/pain/troubles. That is why he wrote with large letters (see Galatians 6:11). One of his main contributions to God's work was writing, and that is where he had problems. Have you ever had problems/troubles in your main ministry for God? Claim the promise of Paul: "God's grace is sufficient for you." So trust in Him. Then Paul said, "his strength was made perfect in weakness" (v. 9). Where have you had the most trouble? Can you claim God's strength to overcome your weakness?

Lord, I pray with Paul for Your grace to work in my weakness. I want You to make Jesus real to me, then help me make Him real to the people to whom I minister. Amen.

Ask with Paul for "the power of Christ to rest upon you." When that happens, you will forget about your pain or problems. You will magnify Jesus. Then pray for others to magnify Jesus with you. You will be so happy when you rejoice with them that you will forget about your suffering, that "thorn in the flesh."

Lord, teach me to pray for others when I suffer. Then help me identify with those I am trying to help. My greatest joy will be Your presence in my ministry. Then my pain will be secondary because I will focus on glorifying Jesus. Amen.

READ:

2 Corinthians 12:1-15

Day 15

WHEN GOD DOESN'T TAKE PAIN AWAY

I was given ... a thorn in the flesh ... three
different times I begged the Lord to take it
away ... He said, "My grace is all you need,
My power works best in weakness."

2 Corinthians 12:7-9, NLT

HAVE you ever asked why you are suffering, whether it is physical or emotional, or the loss of family, friends, or possessions? God has many reasons for allowing it; also He has reasons for the pain's intensity. Paul suffered a "thorn in the flesh" and we don't know exactly what it was. But if God could give one of His best servants—Paul—pain and suffering, then don't question God when He allows pain in your life. You pray for God to take your suffering away; so did Paul—three times. But God did not answer Paul's request, and He may not answer your request to take away your pain. So, if you have pain and your prayer wasn't answered, remember God's answer to Paul: "My grace is sufficient for you."

Lord, forgive me when I complain about my pains; also
forgive me when I complain about You not answering my

prayers. Help me accept Your answer, "My grace is sufficient for you." Amen.

Therefore, your pain will remind you of your human weaknesses. Then claim God's promise: His grace will be made perfect in your hour of pain and weakness. So look away from your pain and look to God, who glorifies Himself by giving health and wholeness to His servants. But He also gives mercy to those suffering in pain.

Lord, I praise You as the Giver. Thank You for giving me answers to my prayers with positive gifts. Also, thank You for not giving me everything I have asked for in the past, because some answers were not in Your will. Amen.

READ:

2 Corinthians 12:1-21

Day 16

WHAT TO DO WHEN SUFFERING

If you are insulted because you bear the name of Christ, you will be blessed, for the glorious Spirit of God rests upon you. If you suffer, however, it must not be for murder, stealing, making trouble, or prying into other people's affairs. But it is no shame to suffer for being a Christian. Praise God for the privilege of being called by his name!

1 Peter 4:14-16, NLT

PETER tells us three positive things about suffering in today's verse. First, "be happy" because your sufferings are evidence that you are saved and the Holy Spirit rests in you. Second, you are not suffering for any crime you have done against society, like murder, but you suffer because you are a Christian who identifies with Christ. Third, it's a privilege to suffer for Christ because He suffered for you in His death on the cross. Then Peter draws the conclusion, "If the righteous suffer, how much more will those who are unrighteous suffer when they are punished for their sins and ungodly ways when they face God at judgment. So look beyond your daily pain and suffering. God knows your predicament. God will help you through it."

Lord, help me focus on You when I suffer pain and loss. Help me see Your encouragement and Your reward. I will live for You—even when I suffer pain—because You will help me get through it now and You will reward me in the future. Amen.

Sometimes our pain is so intense that it demands our whole and immediate attention. You must do what you can to lessen your pain. God doesn't want you to suffer needlessly. But when you cannot get around the pain, always look to God, asking Him to alleviate your pain ... and to help you make it through your pain ... and to glorify Him with your suffering.

Lord, I come to You when I have pain. Teach me how to pray, when to pray, and hear my request. May I become a stronger believer because of my suffering. Amen.

READ:

1 Peter 1:1-6; 4:14-19

Day 17

SUFFERING PREPARES US

Endure suffering along with me, as
a good soldier of Christ Jesus.

2 Timothy 2:3, NLT

THERE are many ways to look at suffering and pain. Think of the hardships endured by a soldier in training: long hikes, physical exercise, controlled diet, sacrifice. Paul reminds us we are in the Lord's army. Therefore, "endure suffering" (2 Timothy 2:3, NLT). The King James translates it "endure hardness." Being a soldier is not easy; it involves sacrifices and hard training. So you are in God's army and there will be times of hardship, suffering, and sacrifice. You do it for Jesus Christ, who suffered for our sins to forgive us. But also you follow the example of Jesus, who gave up all His privileges in Heaven to come suffer for us on Earth.

Lord, thank You for the example of Jesus's sacrificial suffer-
ing. When hard times come, I will not complain, but I will
endure hardness for Jesus. I am a soldier in His army. I will
follow orders. Amen.

When a soldier goes into battle, there are long marches, missed meals, no free time, physical suffering, and even the possibility of death. Will you face the same hardness for Jesus Christ? So prepare for suffering and pain, but enjoy all the good days you have while you can.

Lord, I will prepare for hard days and long nights. I will do what I have to do, and I will suffer what I need to go through—for You. It is a privilege to be Your soldier and follow You. Amen.

READ:

2 Timothy 2:1-26

Day 18

PHYSICAL AND EMOTIONAL PAIN

When he hath tried me, I shall come forth as gold.

Job 23:10, KJV

PERHAPS no one has suffered pain and hurt more than Job. At the beginning of the book of Job, there is a conversation between God and satan. Job lived a prosperous life with lots of money, prosperous farms, and a big family. Satan challenged God to "reach out and take away his health, and he will surely curse you to your face" (2:5). But God was victorious: "... in all this Job did not sin with his lips" (2:10). It's possible to go through the loss of money, property, and family—deep personal pain—and not only learn many things but also glorify God. Then Job lost his health and suffered all types of physical pain. Still Job glorified God. Job demonstrated that it is possible to live through pain and glorify God.

> *Lord, I don't like pain—of any kind. I don't like the pain of*
> *losing things and people, but I will do it for You. I don't like*
> *the pain of losing my health and suffering physical pain, but*
> *I will do it to glorify You. Amen.*

Job lived early in the book of Genesis, and he did not have the advanced revelations that others had, like Moses, the kings, and the prophets. But Job was faithful to his knowledge of God, continually worshipped God, and even praised God for all the things he had been given. As a result, Job became our role model of one who suffered much yet lived for God and glorified Him.

Lord, when I go through sufferings, make me as faithful as Job was. I am not strong now, but strengthen me with the good things I enjoy. Then strengthen me even more with the pain I will suffer in the future. Amen.

READ:

Job 1:1–2:13

Day 19

GRIEF AND EMOTIONAL PAIN

*The words of Nehemiah ... I was in Shushan the
citadel, ... Hanani one of my brethren came with
men from Judah ... and they said to me, "The
survivors who are left from the captivity in the
province are there in great distress and reproach
..." So it was, when I heard these words, that I sat
down and wept, and mourned for many days; I
was fasting and praying before the God of heaven.*

Nehemiah 1:1-4

THIS is a story of grief and emotional pain—not necessarily physical pain. While not physically inflicted, Nehemiah's pain touched his whole life. There may come a time when you will have emotional pain. Nehemiah was grieved that God's city, Jerusalem, was destroyed; so was the temple. He cried for many days. Would you do that? Nehemiah's grief showed his heart for God and the work of God. His grief drove him to fasting and prayer. Nehemiah was a butler and served meals to King Artaxerxes of Persia. Nehemiah's spiritual grief alerted the king, who asked, "Why is your face sad...?" (Nehemiah 2:2). Sometimes your grief will be so severe that it will interrupt your daily activities or even your occupation.

Lord, I will walk close to You, and when terrible news comes, help me get through the ordeal. Help me seek Your presence and come guide me through terrible and trying days. Amen.

King Artaxerxes arranged for Nehemiah to do something about the problem in Jerusalem. Pray that God will give you family and friends to help you get through your pain and grief. When you are walking with Christ and you let the indwelling Christ (see Galatians 2:20) live in you, He will help you through your tragedy. Claim His presence, because Paul said, "I can do all things through Christ who strengthens me" (Philippians 1:21).

Lord, thank You for living in my heart, and thank You for Your assurance and comfort in my life. I may not need Your extra care now, but I will call on You when I need it. Amen.

READ:

Nehemiah 1:1-28

Day 20

MANY KINDS OF HURTS

David mourned for his son [Absalom] every day.

2 Samuel 13:37

But the king covered his face, and the king cried out with a loud voice, "O my son Absalom! O Absalom, my son, my son!"

2 Samuel 19:4

THERE are many kinds of pain, and each pain will give you a different reaction. David's son Absalom had rebelled against David. As the forces of David attacked Absalom and his followers, Absalom was killed. Notice two different experiences of pain by David. First, David loved his son Absalom. The fact his son rebelled and tried to take the kingdom from his father was agonizing to David. But then Absalom was killed. A second type of pain—the agony of death—gripped David when he got the news: "O my son Absalom." David's pure emotion as a father was obvious. But there was a second kind of emotion: the thought that Absalom had sinned and revolted against him and God's plan for Israel. Who can know the heart of a father at a time like this?

Lord, prepare me for painful news that will rock my world, and help me get through my pain and let me see Your plan for my life in all I do. No matter the cause of pain, and no matter how I feel, help me get through it and bring glory to You. Amen.

The human heart can have many feelings and hurts at the same time. David hurt as a father, but also he suffered humiliation because his son rebelled against him. We don't need to analyze David to understand the cause of his pain. We need to sympathize with him and ask God to prepare us for any and all pain/hurt we will experience.

Lord, when pain comes, help me look beyond my hurt to see Your plan for my life. And more than understanding, I need Your presence and comfort. Amen.

READ:

2 Samuel 13:23-39; 19:1-7

Day 21

IDENTIFICATIONAL PAIN

If one part [of the body] suffers,
all the parts suffer with it.

1 Corinthians 12:26, NLT

PAUL described an unusual type of suffering when he wrote that all the parts of the body will suffer when only one part of the body is hurt and suffering. Isn't it true that if your finger is smashed, pain pulsates everywhere? The brain and nerve endings immediately tell every part of your body about the pain. Your hand aches, your whole arm aches, and then your whole body aches and responds. Why? Because the human body is a whole unit, so pain will influence the whole body; obviously it won't hurt in the same way, but everything within the body is aware of your smashed finger. In the same way, when one person in a local body/church is suffering, the church suffers with them. Obviously, not all individuals react the same way with the same intensity, but nevertheless, all are influenced.

> *Lord, give me sensitivity to others in my local body/church*
> *who are suffering. Make me willing to help. Help me do what*
> *I can, the best way possible, with as much as I can. Use me*
> *to help, then give me strength and wisdom to do it. Amen.*

We cannot do everything for everyone we know, but we should do what we can for those hurting in our local body/church. And if we cannot give physical help, at least we can sympathize with them and pray for them. Then our prayers will lead us to any action/response we should make.

Lord, I pray for those in my local body/church who are hurting. Help me do as much as I can, when I can, and continue as long as I should. Lead me and guide me to help those hurting. Amen.

READ:

Luke 10:25-42

Day 22

PAINFUL TO THINK

When I thought how to understand this, it
was too painful for me—until I went into the
sanctuary of God; then I understood their end.

Psalm 73:16-17

THE psalmist tried to understand why evil people prosper and good people seem to suffer on Earth. He said, "it was too painful for me" (v. 16). In the same way, your thoughts can give you pain, as well as physical hurt and/or emotional suffering. It hurt the psalmist to think/remember how sin prospered in the world. God can help us deal with all types of pain, including painful memories: *How did this happen to me?* The psalmist "went into the sanctuary of God" (v. 17). Don't you know that God has an answer for all questions/problems? There are many reasons why you suffer pain, yet those who cheated/lied about you seem to prosper. It is only in God's presence we begin to understand our pain.

Lord, I don't always understand why I have pain. Even if I
don't understand, I will keep my eyes on You and not on the
source of my troubles. I will find my answers in Your pres-
ence, I will find peace and purpose to live, and I will under-
stand Your plan for my life (see Jeremiah 19:11). Amen.

It is painful to think about our problems, failures, and suffering—especially when we cannot do anything about it. So let's do what the psalmist did and "go into the presence of the Lord." Let's focus our attention on Him and His plan for our lives. Only in the Lord will we begin to understand our pain.

> *Lord, teach me to come to You first when I suffer pain. Teach me to find Your answer to why I have pain, and then guide me to pray about my pain. And if it is Your will, give me relief from this pain—both temporarily and completely. Amen.*

READ:

Psalm 73:1-28

Day 23

NO MORE PAIN

*And God shall wipe away all tears from their
eyes; and there shall be no more death, neither
sorrow, nor crying, neither shall there be any more
pain: for the former things are passed away.*

Revelation 21:4, KJV

THERE is a myth that God's children are not supposed to have
pain. Yet there are many things that cause physical pain and
many other causes that bring emotional pain. Pain was promised
in the Garden of Eden, where the first couple sinned. The ultimate pain
was childbirth (see Genesis 3:16). Pain keeps us from hurting ourselves,
and pain teaches us how to do right. Pain warns us of a greater sickness
that is coming, and fear of pain protects us from doing *stupid* things.
Why pain? When God gave us freedom, it involved trial and error, and
with error is pain. We try something and it doesn't work. We hurt ourselves physically, we hurt our bank account, or we hurt our family or the
organization where we work. We may hurt our reputation and ability to
do the things we want to do.

> *Lord, help me understand the nature of pain; then teach
> me many profitable lessons learned from my pain. Teach me
> how to do right and not wrong. Help me learn as much as*

possible, as quickly as possible, so I won't keep making mistakes and hurting myself. Amen.

Today's verse describes Heaven, where we will have no more pain. How wonderful will that be! Why won't we have pain in Heaven? Because we will be smarter and remember more. We will only want to do right things in the right way for the right reasons. And so will everyone else in Heaven. My Sunday school teacher used to say, "Heaven is gonna be a wonderful place. Don't you want to go there?"

Lord, I want to go to Heaven to live with You forever. I want to live where I will not make mistakes and I won't sin. I will do good all the time and praise You. Yes, I want to go there! Amen.

READ:

Revelation 21:1-27

Day 24

REPLACE GRUDGES WITH BLESSINGS

*Bless those who curse you. Pray
for those who hurt you.*

Luke 6:28, NLT

HAS someone mistreated you ... or lied about you ... or cheated you out of money or physical resources? Are you like the world, which gets mad at them ... or gets even with them ... or even seeks revenge? That is not how Jesus would have you respond. You are to bless those who purposefully hurt you. If they curse you, you should pray for them to be saved and follow Christ. Perhaps they spitefully used you; perhaps they cost you time, money, position, and/or dignity. What should you do? Pray for them and/or do good to them. You ask, why do that? Because that is what Jesus would do (see 1 Peter 2:21).

> *Lord, it is hard to pray good things to those who do bad things to me. Change my heart; give me a heart like Jesus. Help me to pray blessings on those who curse me. Help me to pray financial blessings on those who defraud me. Amen.*

God asks you to bless your enemies. He is asking you to do something you cannot do. In the flesh it is natural to retaliate against them.

But God is asking you to respond supernaturally. That means you will do something greater and stronger than you have the ability to do. You need the grace of Jesus to change your attitude. You will need the love of Jesus to show compassion to that person. You will need the grace of God to bless him/her.

Lord, do something powerful for me. Give me Your attitude to pray for my oppressors. Give me a new desire to love and want to help my oppressors. Help me point that person to You and to salvation. Make my oppressors godly people. Amen.

READ:

Luke 6:20-49

Day 25

ACCEPT WHAT YOU CANNOT CHANGE

While the child was alive, I fasted and wept;
for I said, "Who can tell whether the Lord
will be gracious to me, that the child may
live?" But now he is dead; why should I
fast? Can I bring him back again? I shall go
to him, but he shall not return to me.

2 Samuel 12:22-23

DAVID had sex with Bathsheba—not his wife—and sinned against God. They conceived a child who got sick and died. While the child was struggling to live, David fasted and prayed. But when the child died, he quit praying. The principle: accept what you cannot change. Do you have emotional sufferings that cannot be changed? How about physical sufferings that you cannot change? Is it time for you to surrender to God and stop praying for God to take away your pain and suffering? Is it time for you to ask God to help you live with pain? Also, is it time to ask God to teach you lessons from your pain and suffering?

Lord, help me know how to pray about my pain. Should I
stop praying for complete healing? Should I be praying about

lessons to learn from my pain? Show me what to do and how to pray. Amen.

There is one more thing about constant pain. Ask God to glorify Himself through your suffering. You may be a testimony to others in pain, and you may help them endure their pain. Or your courage may motivate them to pray for healing and then get relief. That would be another way for you to be used of God and glorify Him.

Lord, I have asked for healing and that has not come yet. Help me see Your plan for my suffering. Help me be a testimony to others in pain, but most of all, help me bring glory to You. Amen.

READ:

2 Samuel 12:1-25

Day 26

DON'T EXAGGERATE YOUR PAIN

*So David arose from the ground, washed, and
anointed himself, and changed his clothes; and he
went into the house of the Lord and worshiped.
Then he went to his own house; and when he
requested, they set food before him, and he ate.*

2 Samuel 12:20

DAVID was fasting and praying for his child, who was sick and dying. The child was conceived by Bathsheba, who was not married to David. David realized he was being punished for his sin of adultery. As long as the child was struggling to live, David fasted and prayed for healing. But when they told David the child was dead (see 12:19), he quit his fast and stopped praying for the child's recovery. There comes a time when you quit your constant praying over a request. When you know your prayer will not be answered, it is time to stop praying and go on with your life. That is a lesson to all of us when our prayers are not answered. We must move on and give ourselves to God to do what we can do, when we can do it—then do it with all our heart.

*Lord, teach me to be diligent in prayer when my answer can
make a difference. But at the same time, teach me to move*

on to new prayer projects/requests when the time is right to move on. Amen.

Sometimes it is hard to stop praying because there are places in Scripture that exhort us to "pray without ceasing" (1 Thessalonians 5:17). As long as there is hope, pray. As long as God gives you a burden to pray, continue. But when facts tell you there will be no answer, then it is time to move one.

Lord, give me wisdom about how long to pray over a request. I don't want to quit praying too soon. But I also don't want to continue praying when it is obvious my request will not be honored. Amen.

READ:

Psalm 51:1-19

Day 27

WHEN TO QUIT PRAYING

You don't have what you want because you don't
ask God for it. And even when you ask, you don't
get it because your motives are all wrong.

James 4:2-3, NLT

O NE of the first things Jesus taught us about prayer was to "ask and you will receive" (Matthew 7:7, KJV). David asked God to save the life of his son, who was about to die. The son was conceived when David committed adultery with Bathsheba. Were David's motives wrong? Was David covering up his sin with Bathsheba? Was David embarrassed because he was God's king who had been caught in sin? Perhaps no one really knows all that was going on in David's mind. But whatever, God did not answer his prayer, even though David fasted and prayed all night (see 2 Samuel 12:12). So sincerity is not enough to get some prayers answered.

> *Lord, teach me how to pray sincerely—with all my heart.*
> *Also, teach me to pray for the right reason, based on the right*
> *motive, with the right attitude. Then motivate me to pray*
> *with all my heart and to continue till I get an answer. Amen.*

Even though David was sincere and prayed the right way with fasting, God did not answer. We should all learn that God will not answer the wrong prayer request—even if we pray rightly ... sincerely ... continually. This story of unanswered prayer should motivate us to find the right way to pray and then pray rightly.

Lord, teach me when to pray ... how to pray ... and how long to pray. Then, Lord, also teach me when not to pray ... and when to quit praying. Amen.

READ:

James 4:1-17

Day 28

FOCUS ON THE GOOD

*But be sure to fear the Lord and faithfully
serve Him. Think of all the wonderful
things He has done for you.*

1 Samuel 12:24, NLT

DAVID sinned against God by committing adultery with Bath-sheba. As a result the child he conceived got sick. David fasted and prayed for healing, but the child died. Now it was time to do the right thing. David married Bathsheba, and God gave them a child, Solomon. This baby would one day become the next king of Israel. The Bible shows how men (and women) mess up, and when they repent and call on God, He delivers them from trouble ... uses them ... and blesses them. Because David fasted and prayed all night (see 2 Samuel 12:16), God heard and gave David an opportunity to do the right thing.

*Lord, I know You have punished me when I have sinned,
and I repented and called on You for forgiveness. Thank You
for forgiving me. Thank You for a second chance to serve You.
Thank You for using me again in Your ministry. Amen.*

Have you ever messed up and done the wrong thing (sinned)? Have you called on the God of mercy to forgive you? Have you asked the God of the second chance to use you again? Perhaps you could ask Him to use you in a greater way in the future than He has in the past. Think of Peter who denied Jesus—three times—yet God used Peter greatly to preach at Pentecost.

Lord, forgive all my sins. I confess them and plead for Your full restoration. Use me in ministry, even greater than You have in the past. I will serve You gladly and I will testify of Your grace and forgiveness. Amen.

READ:

Mark 14:66-72;

Acts 2:1-14,41-47

PART THREE

FAITH
WALKING
through
SUFFERING & PAIN

LESSONS

Lesson 1:

LEARNING FROM SUFFERING AND PAIN

A. JESUS PROMISED THAT HIS FOLLOWERS WOULD SUFFER TRIALS AND PERSECUTIONS

1. Because of **God, hatred**. "If the world hates you ... it hated Me first" (John 15:18, NLT).

2. Because we follow Jesus. "Since they persecuted Me, they naturally will persecute you" (John 15:20, NLT).

3. Because there are "**worldly desires** that war against your soul" (1 Peter 2:11).

4. Because they "lived that way; following the ... desires ... of our **sinful nature**" (Ephesians 2:3, NLT).

5. Because there are "evildoers" (1 Peter 2:12).

B. WHAT SUFFERING ACCOMPLISHES

1. Suffering conforms us to **Christ**. "Trials will ... purify [your faith] as gold" (1 Peter 1:7, NLT).

2. Suffering **grows** your faith. "Your faith is tested ... grows" (James 1:14).

3. Your suffering helps you **comfort others** who suffer (see 2 Corinthians 1:3-7).

4. Suffering because you follow Christ. "God calls you ... suffering, just as Christ suffered ... follow His steps" (1 Peter 2:21, NLT).

5. Suffering gets **God's attention**. "Since He Himself has gone through suffering ... He is able to help us when we are tested" (Hebrews 2:17-18).

C. WHAT CAN YOU LEARN FROM CHRIST ABOUT SUFFERING?

Develop the **attitude** of Christ when suffering. "Your attitude should be the same that Christ Jesus had ... He did not demand and cling to His rights ... He made Himself nothing ... and in human form He obediently humbled Himself ... by dying a criminal's death on a cross" (Philippians 2:5,7,8).

1. **Yield everything**, as did Christ.

2. Pray, "Your kingdom come in my life, Your will be done."

3. Remember, suffering did not just end Jesus's life; it was the beginning of all things new. Your sufferings can touch/give you **new things**.

4. If you are suffering, keep on **doing what is right** and commit yourself to God.

5. Bitterness and complaining only make you feel worse, **not better**.

6. The joy of doing right can bring more **relief from pain** than wallowing in self-pity and constant complaining. Your complaints will only make you feel worse.

7. In one sense, mind over matter. If you don't mind, it **doesn't matter**. "He will not allow you to suffer above what you are able to bear" (1 Corinthians 10:13, paraphrased).

8. "Let every detail in your lives—words, actions, whatever—be done in the name of the Master, Jesus, thanking God the Father every step of the way" (Colossians 3:17, MSG).

9. Always recognize that God is **in control**.

10. So **yield** the control of your life to Christ.

11. **Never forget**. "You are never alone." "Come, and let us return to the Lord; For He has torn, but He will heal us; He has stricken, but He will bind us up. After two days He will revive us; On the third day He will raise us up, That we may live in His sight. Let us know, Let us pursue the knowledge of the Lord. His going forth is established as the morning; He will come to us like the rain, Like the latter and former rain to the earth" (Hosea 6:1-3).

12. The same providence of God that allowed you to be afflicted can, on the other hand, **relieve** you and **comfort** you.

Lesson 1:

QUESTIONS

LEARNING FROM SUFFERING AND PAIN

A. JESUS PROMISED THAT HIS FOLLOWERS WOULD SUFFER TRIALS AND PERSECUTIONS

1. Because of _____ . "If the world hates you ... it hated Me first" (John 15:18, NLT).

2. Because we follow Jesus. "Since they persecuted Me, they naturally will persecute you" (John 15:20, NLT).

3. Because there are " _____ that war against your soul" (1 Peter 2:11).

4. Because they "lived that way; following the ... desires ... of our _____ " (Ephesians 2:3, NLT).

5. Because there are "evildoers" (1 Peter 2:12).

B. WHAT SUFFERING ACCOMPLISHES

1. Suffering conforms us to _____ . "Trials will ...
    purify [your faith] as gold" (1 Peter 1:7, NLT).

2. Suffering _____ your faith. "Your faith is tested ...
    grows" (James 1:14).

3. Your suffering helps you _____
    who suffer (see 2 Corinthians 1:3-7).

4. Suffering because you follow Christ. "God calls you ... suffering,
    just as Christ suffered ... follow His steps" (1 Peter 2:21, NLT).

5. Suffering gets _____ . "Since
    He Himself has gone through suffering ... He is able to help us
    when we are tested" (Hebrews 2:17-18).

C. WHAT CAN YOU LEARN FROM CHRIST ABOUT SUFFERING?

Develop the _____ of Christ when suffering. "Your attitude should be the same that Christ Jesus had ... He did not demand and cling to His rights ... He made Himself nothing ... and in human form He obediently humbled Himself ... by dying a criminal's death on a cross" (Philippians 2:5,7,8).

1. _____ , as did Christ.

2. Pray, "Your kingdom come in my life, Your will be done."

3. Remember, suffering did not just end Jesus's life; it was the beginning of all things new. Your sufferings can touch/give you _____ .

4. If you are suffering, keep on _____ and commit yourself to God.

5. Bitterness and complaining only make you feel wors, _____ .

6. The joy of doing right can bring more _____ than wallowing in self-pity and constant complaining. Your complaints will only make you feel worse.

7. In one sense, mind over matter. If you don't mind, it _____ . "He will not allow you to suffer above what you are able to bear" (1 Corinthians 10:13, paraphrased).

8. "Let every detail in your lives—words, actions, whatever—be done in the name of the Master, Jesus, thanking God the Father every step of the way" (Colossians 3:17, MSG).

9. Always recognize that God is _____ .

10. So _____ the control of your life to Christ.

11. _____ . "You are never alone." "Come, and let us
    return to the Lord; For He has torn, but He will heal us; He has
    stricken, but He will bind us up. After two days He will revive us;
    On the third day He will raise us up, That we may live in His sight.
    Let us know, Let us pursue the knowledge of the Lord. His going
    forth is established as the morning; He will come to us like the
    rain, Like the latter and former rain to the earth" (Hosea 6:1-3).

12. The same providence of God that allowed you to be afflicted can,
    on the other hand, _____ you and
    _____ you.

HOW TO RESPOND TO SUFFERING AND PAIN

1. The most obvious observation, pain **hurts**!

2. Definition from Webster: (1) "Localized physical suffering associated with bodily disorder or disease or injury." (2) Basic bodily sensation, induced by noxious stimulus, received by naked nerve endings, characterized by physical discomfort and typically leading to evasive actions."

3. Kinds of pain

   a. **Physical** pain. "Her pains came upon her" (1 Samuel 4:19).

   b. **Mental** pain. "It was painful to realize the wicked purpose" (Psalm 73:16, ELT).

   c. **Inter-relationship**. Your physical pain causes worry, fear, grief, and anguish. Your mental pain leads to all types of physical reactions, e.g., headaches, nausea, etc.

   d. C. S. Lewis wrote *The Problem of Pain* (1940) about physical pain when his wife died; he wrote *A Grief Observed* (1961) about mental pain.

4. Kinds of physical pain

    a. Acute pain, **short-term** with easily identifiable causes.

    b. Chronic pain, lasts longer than **normal causes**, i.e., it has outlived its purpose and no longer helps the body prevent injury.

    c. Cutaneous pain, injury to the skin, i.e., **localized pain**.

    d. Somatic pain, from ligaments, bones, blood vessels, i.e., **dull, poorly localized** pain.

    e. Visceral pain, from the body's viscera, or organs. **Hard to diagnose**.

    f. Phantom pain, from a limb that has been lost, but **pain still signals the brain**.

    g. Neuropathy pain, from injury to the nerve system.

5. Kinds of mental pain

   a. Physical **death**. "David mourned for his son every day" (2 Samuel 13:37).

   b. Loss of **dreams or plans**. "When the people heard [couldn't go to Canaan]...they mourned" (Exodus 33:4).

   c. **Memory**. "I sat down and wept and mourned certain days" (Nehemiah 1:4).

   d. **Conviction of sin**. "Be afflicted, and mourn, and weep" (James 4:9, KJV).

   e. **Repentance** of sin. "When ye fasted and mourned ... even those seventy years" (Zechariah 7:5, KJV).

   f. Over **lost life**. "And you mourn at last, when your flesh and your body are consumed" (Proverbs 5:11).

   g. **Deprivation**. "The sufferings of this present time are not worthy to be compared with the glory which shall be ..." (Romans 8:18).

   h. **Identificational pain**. "One member suffers, all the members suffer" (1 Corinthians 12:26).

6. Truths about pain

   a. Pain as **punishment**. "I will greatly multiply thy sorrow ... in sorrow thou shalt bring forth children" (Genesis 3:16, KJV).

   b. Pain is **inevitable**. "Affliction does not come from the dust...yet man is born to trouble, as the sparks fly upward" (Job 5:6-7).

   c. Pain **corrects us** to do right. "A man chasteneth his son so the Lord thy God chasteneth thee" (Deuteronomy 8:5, KJV). "Happy is the man whom God corrects; therefore, despise not the chastening of the Almighty" (Job 5:17).

   d. Pain is one of **God's ministries** to us. "When he hath tried me; I shall come forth as gold" (Job 23:14).

   e. God will **help us** in our pain. "Yea, though I walk through the valley of the shadow of death, I will fear no evil" (Psalm 23:4).

      Fear thou not; for I am with thee: be not dismayed; for I am thy God: I will strengthen thee; yea, I will help thee; yea, I will uphold thee with the right hand of my righteousness. (Isaiah 41:10, KJV)

   f. We must endure **suffering**. "Thou therefore endure hardness [suffer hardship] as a good soldier of Jesus Christ" (2 Timothy 2:3).

   g. You have a **duty to the hurting**. "Weep with them that weep" (Romans 12:15). "Suffer with them as though you are suffering, share the sorrow of those being mistreated, for you know what they are going through" (Hebrews 13:3, ELT).

   h. You get God's **grace and power**. "And he said unto me, My grace is sufficient for thee: for my strength is made perfect in weakness. Most gladly therefore will I rather glory in my infirmities, that the power of Christ may rest upon me" (2 Corinthians 12:9).

7. Attitudes to assume

   a. Since suffering is inevitable, don't think it is unusual. **It happens to all.**

   b. Don't immediately think God is punishing you for a **specific sin**.

   c. Pain **protects** you, for the body shuts down when facing damage.

   d. For some, their suffering is tied to **their sin**. "Sin no more, lest a worse thing come upon you" (John 5:14).

   e. Remember, even Christ had to suffer. "The sufferings of Christ" (1 Peter 1:11).

   f. Don't be ashamed if you suffer **because of your faith** (see 1 Peter 4:16).

   g. Since there is divine purpose for pain, **learn from it**.

   h. Commit your **soul to God** when suffering. "Wherefore let them that suffer according to the will of God commit the keeping of their souls to him in well doing, as unto a faithful Creator" (1 Peter 4:19).

   i. You will leave **this life** in pain. "The pains of death" (Acts 2:24; Psalm 116:3).

HOW TO RESPOND TO SUFFERING AND PAIN

1. The most obvious observation, pain _____ !

2. Definition from Webster: (1) "Localized physical suffering associated with bodily disorder or disease or injury." (2) Basic bodily sensation, induced by noxious stimulus, received by naked nerve endings, characterized by physical discomfort and typically leading to evasive actions."

3. Kinds of pain

   a. _____ pain. "Her pains came upon her" (1 Samuel 4:19).

   b. _____ pain. "It was painful to realize the wicked purpose" (Psalm 73:16, ELT).

   c. _____ . Your physical pain causes worry, fear, grief, and anguish. Your mental pain leads to all types of physical reactions, e.g., headaches, nausea, etc.

   d. C. S. Lewis wrote *The Problem of Pain* (1940) about physical pain when his wife died; he wrote *A Grief Observed* (1961) about mental pain.

4. Kinds of physical pain

  a. Acute pain, _____ with easily identifiable causes.

  b. Chronic pain, lasts longer than _____ , i.e., it has outlived its purpose and no longer helps the body prevent injury.

  c. Cutaneous pain, injury to the skin, i.e., _____ .

  d. Somatic pain, from ligaments, bones, blood vessels, i.e., _____ pain.

  e. Visceral pain, from the body's viscera, or organs. _____ .

  f. Phantom pain, from a limb that has been lost, but _____ .

  g. Neuropathy pain, from injury to the nerve system.

5. Kinds of mental pain

   a. Physical _____ . "David mourned for his son every day" (2 Samuel 13:37).

   b. Loss of _____ . "When the people heard [couldn't go to Canaan]...they mourned" (Exodus 33:4).

   c. _____ . "I sat down and wept and mourned certain days" (Nehemiah 1:4).

   d. _____ . "Be afflicted, and mourn, and weep" (James 4:9, KJV).

   e. _____ of sin. "When ye fasted and mourned ... even those seventy years" (Zechariah 7:5, KJV).

   f. Over _____ . "And you mourn at last, when your flesh and your body are consumed" (Proverbs 5:11).

   g. _____ . "The sufferings of this present time are not worthy to be compared with the glory which shall be ..." (Romans 8:18).

   h. _____ . "One member suffers, all the members suffer" (1 Corinthians 12:26).

6. Truths about pain

   a. Pain as _____ . "I will greatly multiply thy sorrow ... in sorrow thou shalt bring forth children" (Genesis 3:16, KJV).

   b. Pain is _____ . "Affliction does not come from the dust...yet man is born to trouble, as the sparks fly upward" (Job 5:6-7).

   c. Pain _____ to do right. "A man chasteneth his son so the Lord thy God chasteneth thee" (Deuteronomy 8:5, KJV). "Happy is the man whom God corrects; therefore, despise not the chastening of the Almighty" (Job 5:17).

   d. Pain is one of_____ to us. "When he hath tried me; I shall come forth as gold" (Job 23:14).

   e. God will _____ in our pain. "Yea, though I walk through the valley of the shadow of death, I will fear no evil" (Psalm 23:4).

      Fear thou not; for I am with thee: be not dismayed; for I am thy God: I will strengthen thee; yea, I will help thee; yea, I will uphold thee with the right hand of my righteousness. (Isaiah 41:10, KJV)

   f. We must endure _____ . "Thou therefore endure hardness [suffer hardship] as a good soldier of Jesus Christ" (2 Timothy 2:3).

   g. You have a _____ . "Weep with them that weep" (Romans 12:15). "Suffer with them as though you are suffering, share the sorrow of those being mistreated, for you know what they are going through" (Hebrews 13:3, ELT).

h. You get God's _____ . "And he said unto me, My grace is sufficient for thee: for my strength is made perfect in weakness. Most gladly therefore will I rather glory in my infirmities, that the power of Christ may rest upon me" (2 Corinthians 12:9).

7. Attitudes to assume

   a. Since suffering is inevitable, don't think it is unusual. _____ .

   b. Don't immediately think God is punishing you for a _____ .

   c. Pain _____ you, for the body shuts down when facing damage.

   d. For some, their suffering is tied to _____ . "Sin no more, lest a worse thing come upon you" (John 5:14).

   e. Remember, even Christ had to suffer. "The sufferings of Christ" (1 Peter 1:11).

   f. Don't be ashamed if you suffer _____ (see 1 Peter 4:16).

   g. Since there is divine purpose for pain, _____ .

   h. Commit your _____ when suffering. "Wherefore let them that suffer according to the will of God commit the keeping of their souls to him in well doing, as unto a faithful Creator" (1 Peter 4:19).

   i. You will leave _____ in pain. "The pains of death" (Acts 2:24; Psalm 116:3).

Lesson 3:

WHEN PAIN HURTS

A. THREE MYTHS ABOUT PAIN

1. God's children are not supposed to **suffer pain**.

2. If I hurt, there must be something wrong **with me**.

3. If I hurt, there must be something wrong **with God**.

B. WHY PAIN?

1. "If God were good, He would wish to make His creatures perfectly happy, and if God were almighty, He would be able to do what He wished. But the creatures suffer pain; therefore, does God lack **goodness or power**, or both?" (C. S. Lewis)

2. God created us with a **free will**. "God saw that it was good" (Genesis 1:25).

    a. God **surrendered** His free will to control everything.

    b. Man has the power to do all that is intrinsically **possible**, not the impossible.

    c. Man can use his free will foolishly to **produce pain**.

    d. We live in a world of free souls, independent from God.

    e. God decided not to **correct every wrong** independent action when it was done. He decided to wait to see if man's independent nature would choose to love and follow Him.

    f. God intends to give us what we need, not **what we want**.

3. Free will includes the possibility of evil, and men become evil when they do evil.

    a. We think that time cancels sin; since we were not immediately punished, **we think we got away with it**.

    b. We think that if everyone is doing it (sin), it is **normal and okay**.

4. The human spirit will not **surrender to God** as long as all goes well.

5. God can use pain to **bring us to Himself and perfect us**.

   a. Pain insists on being attended to.

      "God whispers to us in our pleasures,
      speaks in our conscience,
      but shouts in our pain." (C. S. Lewis)

   b. Pain shatters our illusion of **self-sufficiency**.

   c. All arguments to justify pain provoke bitter **resentment**.

   d. Christians reject the principle "Being made perfect through suffering" (Hebrews 2:10).

6. Pain is not good in itself but a **tool of God**.

   a. God still fills our life with moments of **joy and pleasure**.

   b. God's **wonderful plan** of Heaven doesn't include pain. "I John saw the holy city ... God shall wipe away all tears from their eyes. And God will wipe away every tear from their eyes; there shall be no more death, nor sorrow, nor crying. There shall be no more pain" (Revelation 2,4). "The sufferings of this present world are not worthy to be compared to the glory that shall be revealed" (Romans 8:18).

C. HOW TO RESPOND TO PAIN

1. Accept what you **cannot change**. "David got up from the ground... he said, 'While the child was still alive, I fasted and wept...but now that he is dead, why should I fast'" (2 Samuel 12:22-23).

2. Don't **exaggerate your pain;** play it down and pray it up. After David's baby died, "he went into the house of the Lord and worshiped" (2 Samuel 12:20).

3. Focus on the **good you have left**, not the bad that was lost. "David comforted his wife...she gave birth to a son and they named him Solomon" (2 Samuel 12:24).

4. People will hurt you, but God **replaces grudges** with blessings. "Bless them that curse you and pray for them which despitefully use you" (Luke 5:22).

   The power of "i": The difference between bitter and better is the letter "i." I can choose how to react.

   "If I allow pain to make me bitter,
   it blinds me to the truth of what God
   wants to do in my life." (Martin Luther)

5. Let God do **His job**. This is earth, where God allows pain for a purpose. This is not Heaven, where He rights all wrongs and eliminates pain.

6. Jesus wants **to heal** our hurting heart.

7. Look **past your pain**. "Elmer, this pain will be a bad dream next week" (Jerry Falwell). "If you would prepare your heart and stretch out your hands toward Him; if iniquity *were* in your hand, *and you* put it far away, and would not let wickedness dwell in your tents; then surely you could lift up your face without spot; yes, you could be steadfast, and not fear; because you would forget *your* misery, and remember *it* as waters *that have* passed away" (Job 11:13-16).

Lesson 3:

QUESTIONS

WHEN PAIN HURTS

A. THREE MYTHS ABOUT PAIN

1. God's children are not supposed to _____ .

2. If I hurt, there must be something wrong _____ .

3. If I hurt, there must be something wrong _____ .

B. WHY PAIN?

1. "If God were good, He would wish to make His creatures perfectly happy, and if God were almighty, He would be able to do what He wished. But the creatures suffer pain; therefore, does God lack
_____ , or both?" (C. S. Lewis)

2. God created us with a _____ . "God saw that it was good" (Genesis 1:25).

   a. God _____ His free will to control everything.

   b. Man has the power to do all that is intrinsically _____ , not the impossible.

   c. Man can use his free will foolishly to _____ .

   d. We live in a world of free souls, independent from God.

   e. God decided not to _____ independent action when it was done. He decided to wait to see if man's independent nature would choose to love and follow Him.

   f. God intends to give us what we need, not _____ .

3. Free will includes the possibility of evil, and men become evil when they do evil.

   a. We think that time cancels sin; since we were not immediately punished, _____ .

   b. We think that if everyone is doing it (sin), it is

       _____ .

4. The human spirit will not _____ as long as all goes well.

5. God can use pain to _____ .

   a. Pain insists on being attended to.

      "God whispers to us in our pleasures,
      speaks in our conscience,
      but shouts in our pain." (C. S. Lewis)

   b. Pain shatters our illusion of _____ .

   c. All arguments to justify pain provoke bitter _____ .

   d. Christians reject the principle "Being made perfect through suffering" (Hebrews 2:10).

6. Pain is not good in itself but a _____ .

   a. God still fills our life with moments of _____ .

   b. God's _____ of Heaven doesn't include pain. "I John saw the holy city ... God shall wipe away all tears from their eyes. And God will wipe away every tear from their eyes; there shall be no more death, nor sorrow, nor crying. There shall be no more pain" (Revelation 2,4). "The sufferings of this present world are not worthy to be compared to the glory that shall be revealed" (Romans 8:18).

C. HOW TO RESPOND TO PAIN

1. Accept what you _____ . "David got up from the ground...he said, 'While the child was still alive, I fasted and wept...but now that he is dead, why should I fast'" (2 Samuel 12:22-23).

2. Don't _____ ; play it down and pray it up. After David's baby died, "he went into the house of the Lord and worshiped" (2 Samuel 12:20).

3. Focus on the _____ , not the bad that was lost. "David comforted his wife...she gave birth to a son and they named him Solomon" (2 Samuel 12:24).

4. People will hurt you, but God _____ with blessings. "Bless them that curse you and pray for them which despitefully use you" (Luke 5:22).

   The power of "i": The difference between bitter and better is the letter "i." I can choose how to react.

   "If I allow pain to make me bitter,
   it blinds me to the truth of what God
   wants to do in my life." (Martin Luther)

5. Let God do _____ . This is earth, where God allows pain for a purpose. This is not Heaven, where He rights all wrongs and eliminates pain.

6. Jesus wants _____ our hurting heart.

7. Look _____ . "Elmer, this pain will be a bad dream next week" (Jerry Falwell). "If you would prepare your heart and stretch out your hands toward Him; if iniquity *were* in your hand, *and you* put it far away, and would not let wickedness dwell in your tents; then surely you could lift up your face without spot; yes, you could be steadfast, and not fear; because you would forget *your* misery, and remember *it* as waters *that have* passed away" (Job 11:13-16).

WHY GOD ALLOWS PAIN

A. GOD IS NOT THE AUTHOR OF PAIN OR SUFFERING

1. God created a perfect man and placed him in a perfect environment.

2. Pain and suffering are the **consequences** of living in a fallen world. "To the woman He said: 'I will greatly multiply your sorrow and your conception; In pain you shall bring forth children; Your desire shall be for your husband, and he shall rule over you.' Then to Adam He said, 'Because you have heeded the voice of your wife and have eaten from the tree of which I commanded you, saying, "You shall not eat of it": Cursed is the ground for your sake; in toil you shall eat of it all the days of your life. Both thorns and thistles it shall bring forth for you, and you shall eat the herb of the field. In the sweat of your face, you shall eat bread till you return to the ground, for out of it you were taken; for dust you are, and to dust you shall return'" (Genesis 3:16-19).

3. The question is not, why do bad things happen to good people? The question is, why do good things happen to bad people?

B. GOD'S ULTIMATE PURPOSE

4. To **be like Jesus**. "For whom He foreknew, He also predestined to be conformed to the image of His Son" (Romans 8:29).

5. God did not create you to be **happy or comfortable**. He created you for a purpose. Advertisements: "live without pain"—this is a myth.

C. GOD SOVEREIGNLY USES PAIN TO FULFILL HIS PURPOSE

1. "God whispers in our pleasures, speaks in our conscience, but shouts in our pain" (C. S. Lewis). Pain is a **loudspeaker**.

2. Pain protects us from **ourselves**.

   a. Physical pain shouts, "*Stop!*"

   b. "And lest I should be exalted above measure ... there was given to me a thorn in the flesh, a messenger of Satan to buffet me, lest I should be exalted above measure" (2 Corinthians 12:7 KJV).

3. Pain strengthens our **character**. "Dear brothers, is your life full of difficulties and temptations? Then be happy, for when the way is rough, your patience has a chance to grow. So let it grow, and don't try to squirm out of your problems. For when your patience is finally in full bloom, then you will be ready for anything, strong in character, full and complete" (James 1:2-4, TLB).

4. Pain strengthens our **faith**. "These trials are only to test your faith" (1 Peter 1:7, NLT).

5. Pain prepares us to **serve Him better**. Joseph was able to feed the world because of what he learned from threats, wrongful imprisonment, lies, and rejections. "You meant evil against me; but God meant it for good" (Genesis 50:20).

6. Pain draws us **closer to Christ**. "That I may know Him and the power of His resurrection, and the fellowship of His sufferings, being conformed to His death" (Philippians 3:10).

7. Pain **awakens us** to strengthen our life purpose. "Therefore, I take pleasure in infirmities, in reproaches, in needs, in persecutions, in distresses, for Christ's sake. For when I am weak, then I am strong" (2 Corinthians 12:10).

8. Pain **motivates us to action**. The pain of a toothache makes us call the dentist. Advertisement for exercise equipment: "no pain, no gain."

9. Pain guides us and teaches us, e.g., **growing pains**. "My troubles turned out all for the best—they forced me to learn from Your textbook" (Psalm 119:71, MSG).

10. Pain may protect us from a **worse situation**.

    a. Fever or infection needs **treatment**.

    b. "For I am ready to fall, and my sorrow is continually before me. For I will declare my iniquity; I will be in anguish over my sin" (Psalm 38:17-18).

Lesson 4:

QUESTIONS

WHY GOD ALLOWS PAIN

A. GOD IS NOT THE AUTHOR OF PAIN OR SUFFERING

1. God created a perfect man and placed him in a perfect environment.

2. Pain and suffering are the _____ of living in a fallen world. "To the woman He said: 'I will greatly multiply your sorrow and your conception; In pain you shall bring forth children; Your desire shall be for your husband, and he shall rule over you.' Then to Adam He said, 'Because you have heeded the voice of your wife and have eaten from the tree of which I commanded you, saying, "You shall not eat of it": Cursed is the ground for your sake; in toil you shall eat of it all the days of your life. Both thorns and thistles it shall bring forth for you, and you shall eat the herb of the field. In the sweat of your face, you shall eat bread till you return to the ground, for out of it you were taken; for dust you are, and to dust you shall return'" (Genesis 3:16-19).

3. The question is not, why do bad things happen to good people? The question is, why do good things happen to bad people?

B. GOD'S ULTIMATE PURPOSE

4. To _____ . "For whom He foreknew, He also predestined to be conformed to the image of His Son" (Romans 8:29).

5. God did not create you to be _____ . He created you for a purpose. Advertisements: "live without pain"—this is a myth.

C. GOD SOVEREIGNLY USES PAIN TO FULFILL HIS PURPOSE

1. "God whispers in our pleasures, speaks in our conscience, but shouts in our pain" (C. S. Lewis). Pain is a _____ .

2. Pain protects us from _____ .

   a. Physical pain shouts, "*Stop!*"

   b. "And lest I should be exalted above measure ... there was given to me a thorn in the flesh, a messenger of Satan to buffet me, lest I should be exalted above measure" (2 Corinthians 12:7 KJV).

3. Pain strengthens our _____ . "Dear brothers, is your life full of difficulties and temptations? Then be happy, for when the way is rough, your patience has a chance to grow. So let it grow, and don't try to squirm out of your problems. For when your patience is finally in full bloom, then you will be ready for anything, strong in character, full and complete" (James 1:2-4, TLB).

4. Pain strengthens our _____ . "These trials are only to test your faith" (1 Peter 1:7, NLT).

5. Pain prepares us to _____ .
   Joseph was able to feed the world because of what he learned from threats, wrongful imprisonment, lies, and rejections. "You meant evil against me; but God meant it for good" (Genesis 50:20).

6. Pain draws us _____ .
   "That I may know Him and the power of His resurrection, and the fellowship of His sufferings, being conformed to His death" (Philippians 3:10).

7. Pain _____ to strengthen our life purpose.
   "Therefore, I take pleasure in infirmities, in reproaches, in needs, in persecutions, in distresses, for Christ's sake. For when I am weak, then I am strong" (2 Corinthians 12:10).

8. Pain _____ . The pain of a toothache makes us call the dentist. Advertisement for exercise equipment: "no pain, no gain."

9. Pain guides us and teaches us, e.g., _____ . "My troubles turned out all for the best—they forced me to learn from Your textbook" (Psalm 119:71, MSG).

10. Pain may protect us from a _____ .

    a. Fever or infection needs _____ .

    b. "For I am ready to fall, and my sorrow is continually before me. For I will declare my iniquity; I will be in anguish over my sin" (Psalm 38:17-18).

PART FOUR

FAITH
WALKING
through
SUFFERING & PAIN

ADDITIONAL RESOURCES

POWERPOINT SLIDES:

To purchase and download the Powerpoint Slides go to
https://www.norimediagroup.com/pages/elmer-towns

VIDEO:

To purchase available video by Dr. Towns go to
https://www.norimediagroup.com/pages/elmer-towns

ADD-ON CONTENT

To purchase additional products in this series go to
https://www.norimediagroup.com/pages/elmer-towns

RELATED BOOKS

My Name is the Holy Spirit: Discover Me through My Name
Available at https://www.norimediagroup.com/pages/elmer-towns

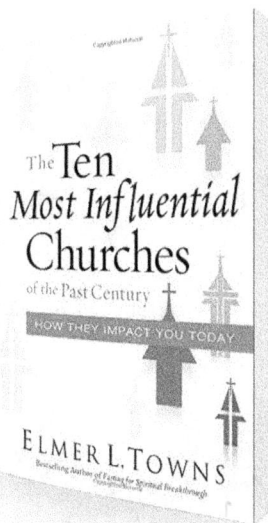

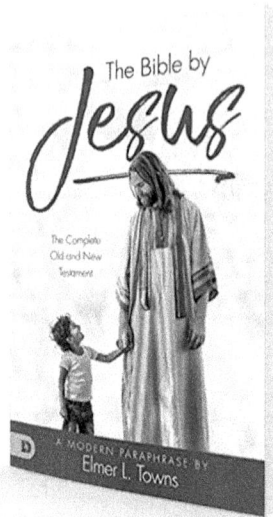

From

ELMER L. TOWNS

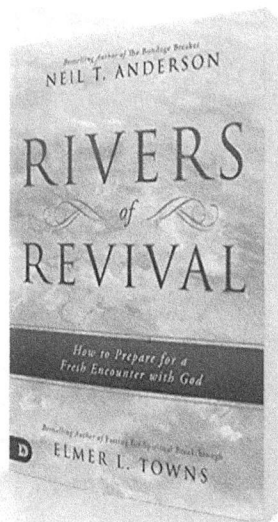

Since the Day of Pentecost, seasons of revival and awakening have brought refreshing to the spiritually dry, life to the spiritually dead, and miraculous encounters with the Holy Spirit.

In this timely and prophetic volume, two bestselling generals of the faith, Dr. Elmer Towns and Dr. Neil T. Anderson, offer collective wisdom, insight, and strategy on how you can experience and release a river of Holy Spirit outpouring into your world!

Additionally, Drs. Towns and Anderson have compiled contributions from other key authorities on revival who have encountered the move of God firsthand. Each contributor provides practical wisdom on how you can experience the Spirit's touch in your own life, church and even geographical region.

A fresh move of God is on the way. Prepare yourself to experience Holy Spirit outpouring like never before!

Purchase your copy wherever books are sold

From

ELMER L. TOWNS

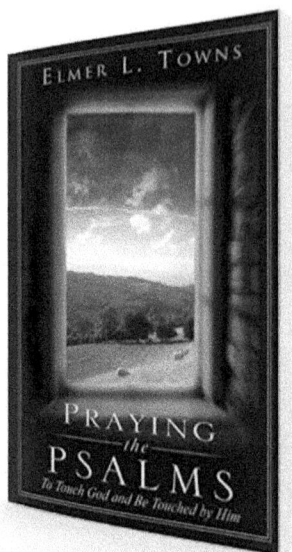

The Book of Psalms reflects the heart of God. *Praying the Psalms* carefully shapes the Psalms into personal prayers enabling you to identify with the Psalmist as he prayed. The author, Dr. Towns, is living breathing testimony of the power and fulfillment you will experience as you read the pages of this most powerful book.

The Psalmist poured our his soul to God concerning the things that deeply moved him. As you read the Psalms, you are taking a peak into his heart. You will weep when he weeps, should when he rejoices, burn when he gets angry and fall on your face when he worships God.

Purchase your copy wherever books are sold

www.ingramcontent.com/pod-product-compliance
Lightning Source LLC
Chambersburg PA
CBHW072150090426
42740CB00012B/2205